De la Tierra

De la Tierra:

The Natural World of Northern New Mexico

by Steve Tapia

Author: Steve Tapia

Cover photo: American Marten, Wikipedia Public Domain

Graphic design: Wink Visual Arts

Copy editing: Matrika Word Services

Published and distributed by: Nighthawk Press, Taos, New Mexico

FIRST EDITION 2015

Library of Congress Control Number: 2015940248

ISBN: 978-0-9862706-3-5

Acknowledgments

With special thanks to my good friend, Diane, who shared in many of the nature experiences I have had and who gave me the idea for a book in the first place.

I also wish to thank *The Taos News*, for giving me an outlet for my passion, and to Judy Esquibel and the other staff with the Taos Public Library for helping with tracking down citations for my articles.

Articles in this work first appeared in *The Taos News* and are reprinted with permission.

Table of Contents

MAMMALS:

FISH:

Introduction

I grew up in an "auto parts" home in Taos; my dad worked at Nixon's Auto Parts beginning in 1958. He worked for over a decade there, until he started Zeke's Auto Supply in '69. He still goes on trips throughout the state selling Western snowplows, while my brother Tracy manages Zeke's Auto Parts. I worked at Zeke's Auto as a kid... until one day when my dad asked me to change the oil in the family car. I started the job in the driveway at home, because my younger brother Carl had an engine all torn apart in the garage and was putting it back together.

So I go ask him for a *really small funnel.* He gives me a funnel but follows me out wondering why I needed a *really small funnel.* Turns out, I was trying to put the clean oil in the dipstick hole. *Nobody ever told me there was an oil fill cap!* I guess it just wasn't intuitive to me! That was my first clue that auto parts just was not my calling. That was 1978. I was 15.

In the summer of '79, I got my first summer job with the Carson National Forest "aqui en Taos" with the Youth Conservation Corp. We cleaned trails and campgrounds, planted trees, built fences and constructed gabions—all sorts of manual labor! That summer, I saw my first bear out in the wild. I saw my first 10-point buck out in the wild. I saw my first flock of wild turkey out in the wild. *I was hooked!*

From then on, I KNEW that I KNEW that I KNEW that natural resource work was what I wanted to do for the rest of my life! I began college at New Mexico State University in Las Cruces, in *Chemical Engineering* of all things! I let the lure of the paycheck get the best of me. The story ends well, though. The following semester I switched to Wildlife Management and have loved what I do ever since.

Do what you love, and you will never work a day in your life!

— Steve Tapia

DE LA TIERRA

Birds

Peregrine Falcon

(Falco peregrinus)

PEREGRINE FALCON

The peregrine falcon, also known as the peregrine, and historically known as the duck hawk in North America, is a widespread bird of prey in the family Falconidae.

A large crow-sized falcon, the male has a blue-gray back, barred white under-parts, and a black head and 'mustache.' The female has similar markings but is all brown in color. As is typical of bird-eating raptors, peregrine falcons are sexually dimorphic, with females being up to 30 percent larger than males.

Fastest Member of the Animal Kingdom

The peregrine is renowned for its speed, reaching over 200 mph during its characteristic hunting 'stoop' (high-speed dive), making it the fastest member of the animal kingdom. The peregrine's breeding range includes land regions from the Arctic tundra to the tropics, which also makes it the world's most widespread bird of prey.

I discovered a peregrine falcon aerie (nest) on a cliff bank on the Pikes Peak Ranger District in Colorado while finishing up Mexican spotted owl surveys in a creek bottom at sunrise. That peregrine went on to achieve fame, as Dr. Jim Enderson from Colorado College fitted him with radio-telemetry and tracked his feeding movements (called 'sorties'). Turns out the peregrine would fly 17 miles one-way for a feeding sortie. The previous distance record was 10 miles.

It just so happened that the Arkansas River was 17 miles southeast of the nest site. The Arkansas River was the hotbed for waterfowl in all of eastern Colorado. Even a bird will go to extreme lengths for a good meal! The scientific name peregrinus is Latin for 'wandering,' reflecting this species' once enormous range over much of the globe and its traveling nature as described above.

The peregrine falcon became an endangered species in many areas because of pesticides, especially organo-chlorine pesticides like DDT. DDT would build up in the falcons' fat tissues, reducing the amount of calcium in their eggshells. With thinner eggshells, fewer falcon eggs survived to hatching. *Oh, what a tangled web we weave!*

Land management agencies, like the U.S. Forest Service, have worked with conservation groups like The Peregrine Fund and many others, to establish 'hack sites,' wherein peregrine chicks are raised in captivity. The chicks are fed through a chute with a hand puppet mimicking a peregrine's head, so that they would not see and imprint on human trainers.

When they are old enough, the rearing box is opened, allowing the young birds to train their wings. As the fledglings get stronger, feeding is reduced, forcing the young birds to learn to hunt on their own.

Worldwide recovery efforts have been remarkably successful. Since the ban on DDT in the early 1970s, populations have recovered, supported by large-scale protection of nesting places and releases of peregrines into the wild, such as through the hacking programs.

Peregrine falcons now nest within the city limits of many urban centers. When I worked in Minnesota, a peregrine falcon pair nested on top of the tallest building in downtown Minneapolis. There was a restaurant on top of that building, and it was a peculiar thing to be eating dinner and have a peregrine falcon whiz by outside the window. Kind of cool, actually.

Wild Turkey

(Melagris gallopavo)

It was to Benjamin Franklin's credit that he thought the wild turkey should be adopted as our national emblem instead of the bald eagle. The turkey was strong, intelligent, wary, and to a certain extent, adaptable. All these attributes have been needed by the wild turkey to enable it to come back from the very brink of extinction to which it had been pushed.

— FROM *GAME BIRDS OF NORTH AMERICA*
BY LEONARD LEE RUE III

WILD TURKEY

In the early days it was a very common bird found throughout most of the country. Wild turkeys were hunted by Native Americans for food, but as the woodland Indians were never very numerous, the hunting pressure was not too great. This pressure greatly increased when Europeans introduced guns to the New World. By the end of the 1800s, most wild turkeys had been wiped out over the vast majority of their range.

With the passage of game laws and their strict enforcement, and the release of turkeys into their historic range(s), the birds have made a remarkable comeback. I worked with the National Wild Turkey Federation in Colorado to release wild turkeys back into their historic range on the Pikes Peak Ranger District. Very gratifying work.

Resilience Defined

From Rue's *Game Birds,* we learn that the wild turkey is a heavy-bodied, stout-legged bird measuring up to 50 inches in length with a wingspan of 50 to 56 inches. The average adult male wild turkey weighs between 14 and 17 pounds, while the female weighs between 8 and 10 pounds. To put this into perspective, consider that the family turkey for last year's Thanksgiving feast is 20 pounds, which goes to show that domestic turkeys and modern-day propagation techniques have changed the rulebook.

The wild turkey's beard has been the source of much argument and the basis for considerable investigation. It is composed of rudimentary bristle-like feathers that are not shed and continue to grow throughout the bird's life. There is one record of a male's beard that was 14 inches long. Kind of like Dusty of ZZ Top. The bigger the beard, the bigger the bragging rights. A caruncle, or wart-like fleshy appendage, protrudes from the middle of the forehead.

There are five subspecies of the wild turkey in the United States. The turkey's original range extended from the Atlantic to the Pacific coasts, and South to North from the Mexican border up to southern Canada. The importation and crossbreeding of these turkeys make it almost impossible to find one of a pure strain today. The wild turkey does not migrate in the true sense of the word, but is subject to seasonal shifts when it changes its range according to food availability, snow depth, or other environmental factors. Being an early riser, the turkey is awake before dawn.

Nowadays the wild turkey, throughout its range, plays a significant role in the cultures of many Native American tribes all over North America. Outside of the Thanksgiving feast, it is a favorite meal in Eastern tribes, both in consumption of the eggs, meat, and turkey 'jerky' (as a means of preserving it to make it last through cold weather). A common practice is controlled burning to create meadow habitat for foraging turkeys, attracting mating birds, and creating clear shooting lanes for hunters. The feathers of turkeys also often made their way into the rituals and headgear of many tribes. Significant peoples of several tribes wore turkey feather cloaks and have ritualistic dances honoring the wild turkey.

Yellow-bellied Sapsucker

YELLOW-BELLIED SAPSUCKER

Although its name sounds like an insult that Yosemite Sam might sling at Bugs Bunny, the yellow-bellied sapsucker's moniker aptly describes its appearance and habits. Both males and females indeed have a pale yellow underside, and tree sap constitutes a large portion of this woodpecker's diet. In fact, sapsuckers have mastered the difficult craft of making sap flow abundantly from trees. This rare ability makes these hardworking master craftsmen a desirable neighbor for many other sap-loving critters, such as ruby-throated hummingbirds, rufous hummingbirds, warblers and nuthatches.

Yosemite Sam's Buddy

The telltale sign of a sapsucker's presence in an area is trees with multiple rows of squarish holes bored into their trunks. Sapsuckers spend hours drilling these holes to get at the sap, which they lap up with their brush-like tongues. I remember living at the Manitou Experimental Forest in Colorado, waking up to the methodical drilling/pecking of the sapsuckers as they went about their work. In this case, the 'dinner host' was a big yellow pine (i.e., mature ponderosa pine).

In the summer, sapsuckers feed on the 'phloem' sap, the sticky fluid that carries the nutrients produced in the needles (or leaves) downward to other parts of the tree. Methodically, the birds begin by making a few horizontal rows of holes. This wounds the tree and causes phloem sap to dam up, accumulating in the plant tissue just above the wound. The holes are enlarged over the course of several days as the sapsuckers extract the sap, and then new ones are added on top of the old, resulting in long vertical lines of holes.

Like any good forester, sapsuckers are selective in using particular trees over others, and they invest a lot of time in managing trees for both current and future use. They often will select individual trees that are wounded or weakened, such as from insects, disease, lightning or wind. The reason for this may be because the sap of trees in poor health contains higher levels of amino acids and protein. Because sap is as vital to trees as blood is to humans, trees have developed means of sealing over wounds to prevent sap from being lost. *Kind of like a tree scab!*

There are two kinds of sap. There is the nutritious phloem, which we've already talked about. Then there is the xylem. Xylem (pronounced *zylem*) is the sap that is readily tapped in early spring for maple syrup in hardwoods in the Northeast. Xylem is a thin liquid that carries water and little nutrients from the roots upwards to the leaves. Unlike the nutritious phloem sap that sapsuckers feed on in the summer, xylem sap is extremely diluted and moves through the tree's vessels more quickly and at higher pressure, and thus flows more freely when tapped.

The yellow-bellied sapsucker is the jet setter of the woodpecker clan. From late March through September, they can be found in young forests in southeastern Alaska, across Canada and the northeastern United States. They have been known to frequent mountainous areas in the fall in New Mexico as well. In the fall, all yellow-bellied sapsuckers take to the skies and travel to the southeastern United States, Mexico, Central America, or the West Indies for the winter. As if taking separate vacations, females tend to travel farther south than males do in the winter. Closely related to the yellow-bellied sapsucker and more common in New Mexico is the red-naped sapsucker. It is often associated with aspen trees, willow and cottonwoods, nearly always nesting in aspen trees.

From a human's perspective, male sapsuckers are thoroughly modern. Not only do they select the breeding territory, choose the nest site, and do most of the cavity excavation, they also pitch in equally to the incubation of the developing eggs and nestlings (even taking the entire night shift) and do most of the nest cleaning. They also do the lion's share of feeding the young.

Sandhill Crane

(*Grus canadensis*)

SANDHILL CRANE

Sandhill cranes are tall stately birds with long necks and fairly long legs. Their tertials (tail feathers) droop over the bird's rump in a 'bustle' that distinguishes cranes from herons. Cranes fly with their neck and legs fully extended. The courtship rites include a frenzied, leaping 'dance' of sorts, which makes it quite unique.

The adult sandhill crane is gray overall with dull red skin on the crown and lores (nostrils); a whitish chin, cheek and upper throat; and blackish primary feathers. The immature cranes lack the red patch, and the gray body is irregularly mottled with a brownish-red hue. According to National Geographic's *Birds of North America*, full adult plumage is reached after 2.5 years.

The Noblest Fliers

The sandhill crane is locally common, and breeds on tundra and in marshes and adjacent grasslands in Canada and the Northwest Territories. They migrate south for the winter, and regularly feed in dry fields in southern Colorado and northern and central New Mexico. The Monte Vista National Wildlife Refuge in the San Luis Valley of southern Colorado is a favorite stopover for seeing sandhill cranes in the fall and winter months and can be easily observed during these times. In their wintering areas they form flocks of over 10,000 birds. Another place to observe this wonder is at the Bosque del Apache National Wildlife Refuge about 100 miles south of Albuquerque, New Mexico.

The common call of the sandhill crane is a trumpeting, rattling *gar-oo-oo* and is audible for more than a mile. In "Crane Music," writer Paul Johnsgard describes this as follows: "Cranes are the stuff of magic, whose voices penetrate the atmosphere of the world's wilderness areas."

From Johnsgard, we learn that cranes generally migrate by day, and also typically organize into coordinated formations during such flights. Edward Topsell (1572–1625) believed that "the foremost bird in such a formation acted as 'captain,' and that all the subordinate birds of the group organized themselves in such a way as to avoid obscuring its view." Various older birds would take turns at being the flock leader.

While flying, and especially during landings and takeoffs, cranes utter a constant clamoring, enabling pair and family members to maintain vocal contact amid the confusion of flock movements. Kind of like one of our Maestas' family reunions, which regularly numbers between 175 and 200 people. We must be doing something right: it's our family reunion's 30th anniversary next year!

When lone birds have somehow been separated from their social groups, it is common to see them flying back and forth over roosting flocks calling almost constantly. The 'unison call' is a complex and extended series of notes uttered by paired birds in a time-coordinated sequence. The unison call and its associated vocalizations are typically the loudest and most penetrating of any species' calls. *Ain't nature grand!*

Sandhill cranes have been used as foster parents for endangered Whooping Crane eggs and young 'whooper' re-introduction efforts for that species. This project failed as these foster-raised Whooping Cranes imprinted on their parents and later did not recognize other Whooping Cranes as their 'kind'—attempting instead, unsuccessfully, to pair with Sandhill cranes.

Osprey

(*Pandion haliaetus*)

OSPREY

This is a fish-eating bird of prey, also called a sea hawk or a fish hawk. It is a large raptor reaching more than 24 inches in length with a 71-inch wingspan. This is a *big* hawk. It is brown on its upper parts and predominately greyish-white on the head and lower parts with a black eye patch and wings. The iris of the eye is golden-brown with a transparent nictating membrane that is pale-blue in color. The bill is black with a blue cere (nostrils), and the feet are white with black talons. A cool-looking bird!

The Fish Eagle

The osprey tolerates a wide variety of habitats, nesting in any location near a body of water providing an adequate food supply. Fish make up 99 percent of the osprey's diet. It is found on all continents except Antarctica, although in South America it occurs only as a non-breeding migrant. As its common name(s) suggest, the osprey's diet consists almost exclusively of fish, and it possesses specialized physical characteristics and exhibits unique behaviors to assist in hunting and catching its prey.

Ospreys have been known to exhibit great joint flexibility. An example of this is when flying toward bright light, such as the sun, they are able to bend the joint in their wings to shield their eyes from the light to fly safely. Also, ospreys have reversible toes with sharp 'spicules' (little spikes) on the underside of their toes to help them hold onto their catch. *Ain't nature grand!*

The sexes appear fairly similar, however the adult male can be distinguished from the female by its slimmer body and narrower wings. The breast band of feathers on the male is also weaker in coloration when compared to that of the female or non-existent altogether. The juvenile osprey may be identified by buffy white fringes on the plumage of the under-parts and streaked feathers on the head.

The capture method of ospreys consists of initial visual scanning from above the water, often after a period of active hovering, flapping or gliding, depending on the wind, and at heights ranging from 5 to 70 meters (roughly 5 to 230 feet). Most dives are made from about 20 to 30 meters (roughly 65 to 100 feet) above water. At times the bird may skim horizontally over the water and snatch a fish. Site fidelity to a particular aerie (nest site) appears to be strong, and a long-term pair bond is often typical for the species. During pair formation, the male may soar and make undulating dives above the nest site, either alone or with the female. This display is sometimes called the "sky-dance song-flight," and often begins and ends at the aerie.

One apparently unique display is for the male to flap his wings vigorously while high above the ground, at the same time dangling his feet, sometimes holding a fish, and calling in a frenzied manner. During this display he may even fly backward. Show off!

The display is not only directed toward females as a courtship display but also apparently intended to distract intruders. Paul Johnsgard in *Hawks, Eagles and Falcons of North America* said sky dances seem to mark out nesting territories as well as advertise the aerie to females, and that intruding males may be "escorted away" by the male. Re-use of old nest sites is regular in ospreys, although the old nests are "renovated", and new materials are added.

Western Tanager

(*Piranga ludoviciana*)

WESTERN TANAGER

Stan Tekiela in *Birds of New Mexico* describes the Western tanager as a canary yellow bird with a red head; black back, tail and wings; and one white and one yellow wing bar. It truly does look like a bird that escaped from the local wild bird shop, but they are common throughout most of New Mexico. The males' stunning breeding plumage is not to be forgotten.

This is the farthest nesting tanager species, reaching up into the Northwest Territories of Canada. Paul Sterry and Brian E. Small describe it in their book *Birds of Western North America* as a colorful, plump-bodied songbird, whose unobtrusive habits make it easily overlooked (believe it or not), but to see one is to remember it forever. There are three species of tanager in the West, and each is equally colorful. Each bird migrates to Central America in winter, except for the Hepatic tanager, which winters mainly in Mexico.

This is a good time to ask the question why the males of most bird species are more colorful than the females of the same species, as is the case with this songbird. And no guys, the answer is *not*: "Well, dudes are just better-lookin'!" The answer lies in something called 'sexual dimorphism.' It means, well: "Dudes are just better-lookin'!" Ha-ha!

Sexual dimorphism means the female of the species selects the "fittest" male of the same species to have their young with. We can thank Mr. Charles Darwin for that 'ain't nature grand' moment, which he wrote about in his 1871 *Theory of Natural Selection* book used by scientists young and old throughout the world. Sexual dimorphism is a product of both genetics and environmental factors.

Turkey Vulture

(*Cathartes aura*)

Turkey vultures are masters of using updrafts and thermals: they are capable of teasing lift from the skies even when all other soaring birds are grounded. With their wings angled slightly upward forming a V-shape, turkey vultures rock from side to side catching rising air as they migrate along the slopes of the Rockies.

TURKEY VULTURE

The head of a turkey vulture is naked, and as a result, the bacteria and parasites they encounter while digging in rotting carcasses can be easily cleaned off. Vultures eat carrion almost exclusively; their bills and feet are not designed to crush or kill living animals. Chris Fisher in *Birds of the Rocky Mountains* said recent genetic studies have shown that turkey vultures are most closely related to storks, not hawks and falcons.

Turkey vultures do not build nests. The eggs, typically two, are laid in a depression on the ground, on a cliff ledge, or in a cottonwood tree. The cliff ledges adjacent to the Rio Grande River make a perfect nesting place for the turkey vulture. Vultures typically migrate to Central and South America for the winter, often returning to their spring roosts on the same day every year at around the vernal (spring) equinox.

The Clean-up Crew

The Cherokee Indian name for this bird is 'peace eagle,' perhaps because it does not typically kill its food. In *Winging It: A Beginner's Guide to Birds of the Southwest*, Hilaire Bellox states that the vulture "eats between meals, and that is the reason why he very, very rarely feels as well as you or I. His eye is dull, his head is bald, his neck is growing thinner… Oh, what a lesson for us all to eat only at dinnertime."

The turkey vulture's digestive system kills the viruses and bacteria in the food that it eats. Its droppings and regurgitated pellets, called *bolus,* have been studied and are found to be "clean" and do not carry disease. Miraculous, considering the turkey vulture lives on the decaying bodies of dead animals. That makes this scavenger a member of the 'clean-up crew' A-Team!

The Birds and the Bees

Bees in Northern New Mexico

HONEY BEE

There are two major pollinators of native plants and crops in Northern New Mexico: hummingbirds and bees. This is the story of the bees. Over 500 species of bees have been reported from New Mexico.

Many of these bees pollinate native flowers, and some of them also pollinate crops such as fruit trees. We know how to manage only a handful of bee species. The blue orchard bee, *Osmia lignaria*, has been used successfully on a limited scale for pollination of almonds, apples, cherries, and prunes. A related species, *O. ribifloris*, shows promise as a pollinator of blueberries.

Most Osmia species are ground-nesting and docile. The New Mexico Pollinator Project is identifying potentially important crop pollinating native bees in New Mexico, and works to preserve, increase, and where possible, manage native bee populations.

Why use native bees for crop pollination? 1) They are docile. 2) They are efficient pollinators, so few bees are needed (~250 females / acre). 3) They are more active in poor weather. 4) They are not active after bloom, so pesticides have a limited effect. 5) Pollination by native bees may compliment honeybee activity. 6) They are one of the State's natural resources and should be conserved.

Ken Hays, President of the New Mexico Beekeepers Association, says New Mexico's bees are faring better than in most places around the world, including the neighboring states of Colorado and Texas, where instances of the phenomenon known as bee colony collapse are decimating hives and putting beekeepers out of business.

Longtime master beekeeper and former New Mexico State Bee Inspector Les Crowder concurs, saying New Mexico bees in general are healthier than in other states for a couple of reasons: 1) development of a strong New Mexico breed, and 2) the fact that few beekeepers travel to other states to hire out their hives for pollination.

Hays says pesticides can wipe out hives, especially by aerial spraying. He advises beekeepers to place beehives near protected areas, such as near water sources and/or near flowering plants. And, Hays is convinced hives must be kept away from genetically modified crops. "That's where you see colony collapse," he says. The only hives he's lost to die-off were 20 hives situated next to fields of genetically modified corn.

Instead of harrowing between rows, the farmer will use an herbicide to kill weeds. The implication for bees is that "the pollen becomes poison and kills the insects," Hays says. Once again: *Oh, what a tangled web we weave.*

Recognizing that colony collapse threatens about one-third of the nation's food sources, Congress has put $75 million specifically toward funding research into the causes of colony collapse. Fully one-third of the crops we eat will not grow without pollination. On a positive note, Les Crowder stated, "Bees this year look better than ever. To me, it's not the doom and gloom situation it is for commercial beekeepers. Small-scale and feral bees (at least in New Mexico) are OK."

The last major issue is in regards to the African killer bees. As of 2002, Africanized honeybees have spread from Brazil south to northern Argentina and north to Central America, Trinidad, Mexico, Texas, Arizona, New Mexico, Florida, and now Southern California. In June 2005, they were also discovered in southwest Arkansas, and in September 2007 they established themselves in the vicinity of New Orleans, Louisiana.

Scaled Quail

(*Callipepla squamata*)

SCALED QUAIL

The scaled quail, also commonly called blue quail or cottontop, is a bluish-gray bird that lives in the arid regions of the Southwestern United States down to Central Mexico. This bird is named for the scaly appearance of its breast and back feathers, and is easily identified by its white crest that resembles a tuft of cotton on top of its head, hence the reason old-timers called it 'cottontop.'

I always loved the scientific name of this bird. My pet name for my college girlfriend was "my little callipepla." *OK, OK, I'm a freak!* Scaled quail inhabit dry open valleys, plains, foothills, rocky slopes, draws, gullies and canyons that have a mixture of bare ground, low herbaceous growth, and scattered brushy cover. In short, good scaled quail habitat is characterized by low-growing grasses with forbs and shrubs. Scaled quail avoid dense growth associated with the sides of streams, but an absolute requirement is a source of open water. There is some debate in the literature as to whether there really is such a requirement.

Ole Cottontop

The most well-known trait of this bird is, when disturbed, it prefers to run rather than fly. The bird will find a bush to hide in, like sagebrush or rabbit brush, rather than continue to run. Scaled quail are opportunistic eaters. Seeds are consumed year-round, especially hackberry, Russian thistle, rough pigweed, sunflower, ragweed, or really whatever is available. They aren't choosy. J.S. Ligon stated in his book *New Mexico Birds and Where To Find Them* that the distribution of scaled quail is largely coextensive with mesquite, condalia, and cholla cactus.

Scaled quail lay from nine to 16 eggs. Eggs are incubated by the female for 21 to 23 days, and double brooding (the production of two consecutive broods in one season) is fairly common. The precocial young (alert at birth) leave the nest shortly after hatching, but are accompanied by at least one or sometimes both parents, who show them how to find food. The young quail fledge rapidly and are adult in size in 11 to 15 weeks.

Scaled quail are fairly sedentary, and the home ranges of separate "coveys" (small family groups) overlap only slightly or not at all. In the winter, coveys of quail have home ranges varying from 24 to 84 acres, and the average winter covey size for scaled quail is around 30 birds, although coveys of up to 150 birds have been reported. In New Mexico, predators on scaled quail include hawks, owls, coyotes and snakes.

Scaled quail populations seem to have declined sharply across their range in past decades, though this species' boom-and-bust population cycles make it hard to accurately estimate long-term trends. Ways to improve habitat for scaled quail include leaving fields fallow for a season, allowing weeds to grow up, and/or creating brush piles. I would not provide supplemental food in the form of grains, as this method becomes too expensive to be practical.

Pinyon Jay

(*Gymnorhinus cyanocephalus*)

PINYON JAY

A highly social bird of the lower mountain slopes of the western United States, the pinyon jay is specialized for feeding on pine seeds. Each jay stores thousands of seeds each year and has such a good memory that it can remember where most of them were hidden. The pinyon jay can find seeds that it hid even under the cover of snow.

It is aided by a relatively long, strong bill, an expandable throat, and long, strong wings. Mated pairs of pinyon jays appear to coordinate their caching of seeds so that their cache location is known to each other and to other members of the flock. As I mentioned, this species is highly social. The pinyon jay can form flocks of 250 or more birds, and several birds seem to act as sentries for the flock, watching out for predators while their companions are feeding.

Social Bird with a Great Memory

The nest is always part of a colony, but there is never more than one nest per tree. There are usually three to four eggs laid, quite early in the season (January or early February), and incubation is usually 16 days. The young are normally fed only by their parents, but once they are nearly ready to leave the nest, they can sometimes receive a meal from any member of the colony. One might say that 'birds of a feather flock together.'

Breeding activities, from nest building to the feeding of the young, are related to the availability of conifer seeds. In years when bumper crops of pinyon seeds are available, pinyon jays have the opportunity to breed twice. When the pinyon crop fails, pinyon jays forego late-winter breeding and instead breed in August when crops of pinyon seeds are ripe. "Courtship parties," consisting of all adult birds in the flock, are formed. Pinyon jays in these courtship parties fly several miles away from the group foraging area to breed in a *new* colony.

Pinyon jays appear to be highly adaptive. For example, pinyon jays learned to modify their nest site location based on prior experience. Following at least two encounters with predators, pinyon jays learned to avoid building their nests in exposed areas of trees. In general, adults have a better chance of survival than yearlings, and yearlings have a better chance of survival than young-of-the-year.

Pinyon jays interact in a mutual relationship with pinyon trees. Pinyon trees provide pinyon jays with food, nesting and roosting sites, and breeding cues. Pinyon jays influence seed dispersal, seed establishment, and genetic structure of pinyon populations.

Pinyon jays are in the same family of birds as crows, ravens, magpies, and nutcrackers. As a group, they are considered among the most intelligent of all animals. Their brain-to-body mass ratio is equal to that of great apes and only slightly lower than humans. Folklore often represents corvids as clever, and even mystical animals. Some Native Americans believed that a raven created the earth. Despite also being known as a trickster spirit, ravens were popular on totems, credited with creating man and responsible for placing the sun in the sky. Later, in Western literature, popularized by American poet Edgar Allen Poe's work "The Raven," the common raven becomes a symbol of the main character's descent into madness.

Chickadees

(*Poecile Genus*)

CHICKADEES

"My Little Chickadee" is the catchphrase most associated with Mae West and W.C. Fields taken from the 1940 comedy/western movie by the same title. I was just a kid in diapers when it came out on *"Dialing for Dollars,"* but I do remember.

Chickadees are almost universally considered 'cute', thanks to its oversized round head, tiny body, and curiosity about everything, including humans. My good friend Diana—"The Lady Di"—got to experience this firsthand when a black-capped chickadee ate from her hand when she was outside filling up the bird feeders. One of life's simple joys and fond memories.

Another fond memory I have of this little bird occurred during my first bow-hunting adventure when I lived in Wisconsin. I was perched in a tree stand up in the treetops when a black-capped chickadee began to crawl up my leg—until he figured out I wasn't a tree! Here was my first clue that my attempt to 'fit in with nature' was probably working.

The black cap and bib and white cheeks of the black-capped chickadee readily identify this small bird over most of its widespread range. Similar to it is the mountain chickadee, which is a handsome little gray bird with a black cap and throat and a white stripe above the eyes, or as my sister Sandra says, "Oh, you mean the one with the white eyeliner?" Smaller than a sparrow, it is found in ponderosa pine, spruce-fir, and piñon-juniper forests. Chickadees stay year-round, although some young birds will migrate, and some birds will go to lower elevations in the winter.

Rocky Mountain forms of the mountain chickadee are tinged with buff on their back, sides, and flanks and have broader white eyebrows. The call is a coarse *chick-adee-adee-adee.* Typical song is a three- or four-note descending whistle *fee-bee-bay* or *fee-bee fee-bee* (*Birds of North America,* National Geographic).

The black-capped chickadee call is a lower, slower *chick-a-dee-dee-dee-dee* or a clear, whistled *fee-bee-ee,* with the first note higher in pitch. Where their ranges overlap, as in Taos, the two species may hybridize.

Chickadees can go into a state of very low body temperature to conserve energy during the winter, and while in this slowed sluggish state the birds can still fly, but not very fast or very far. The white eyebrow above the eye and pale gray sides distinguish the mountain chickadee from other chickadees such as the black-capped chickadee, which can also be found in Taos and in extreme northern New Mexico. In fact, I just saw some black-capped chickadees the other day. Altitude separates the two cousins, with mountain chickadees living at higher elevations in the Western mountains.

They are very active and acrobatic, clinging to small limbs and twigs or hanging upside down from pinecones. In winter, mountain chickadees flock with kinglets and nuthatches, with birds following each other one by one from tree to tree. Mountain chickadees prefer the dry mountainous forests of the West, while their cousins the black-capped chickadees stick to evergreen trees on higher slopes.

Insects (especially caterpillars) form a large part of their diet in the summer, and seeds and berries become more important in the winter. Black-oiled sunflower seeds are readily taken from bird feeders and even from your hand, which is one of my fondest memories of living at the Manitou Experimental Forest in Colorado. Chickadees will take a seed in their bill and fly from the feeder to a tree, where they proceed to hammer the seed on a branch to open it.

So next time you see a chickadee, black-capped or mountain, go outside with a handful of seed, stand perfectly still with your arm outstretched, and see if you can get one to land on your hand and take a seed. I tell you, it's one of life's simple pleasures!

Mallard

(*Anas platyrhynchos*)

MALLARD

Probably the best-known and most abundant wild duck in the Northern Hemisphere, the Reader's Digest *Book of North American Birds* lists the mallard as the ancestor of almost every breed of domestic duck in North America. Tekiela's field guide describes the mallard's unique color combination with bulbous green head, white necklace, chestnut-colored chest, gray and white sides, yellow bill, and orange legs and feet. That's quite a cornucopia of color but perfectly describes the male mallard duck.

A familiar duck of lakes, ponds, swamps and rivers, like the Rio Grande, the mallard is considered a 'dabbling duck,' meaning it tips forward in shallow water to feed on aquatic plants on the bottom. Stan Tekiela's field guide tells us that the name mallard comes from the Latin *masculus*, meaning 'male', referring to the habit of males not taking part in raising ducklings. In the wild it is an opportunistic feeder, eating snails, aquatic insects, grasshoppers, fish eggs, and aquatic vegetation—practically anything it happens to find.

Green Heads

But given a choice, the mallard will feast on seeds day after day, and as a result, its flesh is usually quite palatable. Little wonder, then, that Reader's Digest reported in 1990 that mallard was a valued addition to poultry yards on three continents—where it provides people with eggs, meat, down and feathers in almost limitless abundance.

In North America it summers across most of Canada and the United States, and its winter range extends well into Central America. Still, no matter how great its numbers in the wild, or how widespread its distribution, the mallard continues to be known as a 'domestic duck' almost everywhere. And the loud, resonating, down-the-scale QUACK of the female mallard has become, perhaps more than any other, *the* call that sounds 'duck' to people the world over.

The mallards' nest is a down-lined hollow of grass and stems hidden in the vegetation near water. I fondly remember 'nest-dragging' at the Sherburne National Wildlife Refuge in central Minnesota. We pulled a 20-foot rope with tin cans tied to it between two ATVs in an attempt to flush nesting ducks. It raised a real ruckus! The hens would sit on the nest until the last second before flying off and revealing their nest location. We would then record the species of duck, count the number of eggs in the nest, and approximate how many days until hatching (through a procedure called 'candling').

The hen lays five to 14 white to pale-green eggs, and incubates them for 26–29 days before they hatch. The ducklings leave the nest soon after hatching, and first fly at about eight weeks of age. You *don't ever* want to accidentally run over a nest with your ATV while nest-dragging: you won't sleep for a week.

Somehow, perhaps by sensing changes in atmospheric pressure, birds can perceive the approach of major weather systems. This is the "instinctive perception" about which Aristotle wrote, according to Weidensaul in *Living on the Wind: Across the Hemisphere with Migratory Birds*. But environmental triggers like photoperiod (daylength) and weather will not, of themselves, prompt a bird to migrate. There is a genetic component as well. Bird migration is one of the most riveting and miraculous phenomena on the planet.

Magpies, Crows, and Ravens

(Anas platyrhynchos)

Oh My! The Corvids

The beauty of the magpie (*Pica pica*) is too often overlooked because of its raucous and aggressive demeanor that overshadows its gorgeous, panda-like plumage. Tekiela's *Birds of New Mexico* describes their wings and tail as beautiful, iridescent green in direct sunlight. The long shiny tail of the black-billed magpie, a member of the Corvid family, is one of the longest of any North American bird. Most residents are jaded by the omnipresence of magpies, but foreign visitors to Taos are often captivated by their beauty and approachability.

MAGPIE

The abundance of hooved mammals, road kill and jackrabbits in Northern New Mexico provides magpies and other scavengers with a dependable food source during hard winters, and serve as fundamental building blocks for the Rocky Mountain food web.

They are very intelligent and able to mimic dogs, cats, people, and other birds, according to Tekiela. They eat primarily carrion, insects, fruit and seeds. They are very gregarious, travel in small flocks, and usually mate with the same female for several years. They typically have a dome-shaped roof over a nest platform within thick shrubs, or sometimes apple orchards. I say this because that's where I first learned about nesting magpies—in the Pacheco's apple orchard. It was next to the road where as kids we would run away from *La Llorona* at dark… But that's a different story!

Magpies can recognize themselves, unlike say, robins. Shine a red dot onto a magpie's breast, and it will carefully look in a mirror and then preen its own breast feathers in search of the apparent wound. A black dot shone on the same feathers does not produce such alarm. This demonstrates self-awareness and explains the ability of magpies to recognize and discriminate social partners. Recognizing social companions allows magpies, crows and ravens to save time and energy by hiding food and other resources only from potential thieves.

Close relative to the magpie is the American crow *(Corvus brachyrhynchus).* In Candace Savage's *Bird Brains: The Intelligence of Crows, Ravens, Magpies, and Jays*, we learn that the Rev. Henry Ward Beecher (mid-1800s) once said, "If men had wings and bore black feathers, few of them would be as clever enough to be crows." These native birds are wary, highly intelligent birds capable of solving simple problems that make them excel at self-preservation.

Aesop's *The Crow and the Pitcher* fable, also included in Savage's book, gives some insight into the intelligence of crows:

> A thirsty Crow found a pitcher with some water in it, but so little was there that, try as she might, she could not reach it with her beak, and it seemed as though she would die of thirst within sight of the remedy. At last she hit upon a clever plan. She began dropping pebbles into the Pitcher, and with each pebble the water rose a little higher until at last it reached the brim, and the knowing bird was enabled to quench her thirst.

Webster defines 'flexibility' as the ability to perceive relationships and use one's knowledge to solve problems and respond appropriately to novel situations. Given Aesop's fable above, it is safe to say that crows are very flexible! In the fall, after breeding, American crows group together in flocks of thousands, called a "murder"—a term that is understandable to those who have seen Alfred Hitchcock's *"The Birds"*—but *the* aggregation is merely a get-together in preparation for an evening flight to the roost...kind of a family reunion of sorts!

The American crow is a non- to partial migrator that often stores bright, shiny objects in its nest. My best friend as a kid found his new glasses in that very same nest I referred to earlier. The American crow often re-uses the same nest every year, and they live up to 20 years. So, as you can imagine, the nests can get fairly large. One of the smartest of all birds, and very social, often entertaining itself by provoking chases with other birds, or the family dog for that matter, the American crow feeds on road kill but rarely is hit by a car.

Corvus brachyrhynchus (American crow), despite sounding cumbersome, in Latin means "raven with a small nose," which brings us to our next member of the family Corvidae. There is nothing common, though, about the common raven (*Corvus corax*)!

Glorified in traditional cultures worldwide, the common raven does not act by instinct alone. Whether tumbling aimlessly through the air, delivering complex and meaningful vocalizations, or sliding playfully down a snowy bank on its back, this raucous bird demonstrates behavior many think of as being exclusively human.

Few birds naturally occupy as large a natural range as the raven, but the Rocky Mountains remain one of the most reliable places in which to experience their habits. It seems that little goes on in the Rockies without the omnipresent raven surveying the scene. The raven mates for life, and they occupy the same nest for many years.

The main difference between a raven and a crow is that the raven is about 22 to 27 inches, as opposed to a crow's 18 inches. They also have shaggy feathers on the chin and throat whereas the crow does not, and the low raspy call of a raven is different from the higher-pitched call of the crow. The raven's diet is carrion, insects, fruit, and occasionally small mammals, and it is also a non- to partial migrator. In this respect, they mirror the American crow.

To sum up, members of the crow and raven family Corvidae, are perhaps second only to house sparrows and pigeons, as the most prominent features of urban landscapes in much of the world. We create the road kill and garbage that they love to devour; they are even likely to snatch your fast-food hamburger from the picnic table, undeterred by its lethal fat content. Not only do corvids tend to thrive in human-made environments, but they have also penetrated our psyches. We 'eat crow,' climb to the top of a 'crow's nest,' tear things apart with a 'crowbar,' and are 'ravenous' after a long hike without food. Let your mind wander a bit and consider our language, art, culture and religion. They have all been influenced over the ages by our interactions with ravens and crows.

RAVEN

While on a lecture tour in India in 1896, Mark Twain was besieged by flocks of house crows as he ate, smoked and wrote. Twain's description of the species as an accumulation of many incarnations perfectly suits all crows:

> In the course of his evolutionary promotions, his sublime march toward ultimate perfection, he has been gambler, a low comedian, a dissolute priest, a fussy woman, a black guard, a scoffer, a liar, a thief, a spy, an informer, a trading politician, a swindler, a professional hypocrite, a patriot for cash, a reformer, a conspirator, a rebel, a royalist, a democrat, a practitioner and propagator of irreverence, a meddler, an intruder, a busybody, an infidel, and a wallower in sin for the mere love of it.
>
> The strange result, the incredible result, of this patient accumulation of all damnable traits is, that he does not know what care is, he does not know what sorrow is, he does not know what remorse is, his life is one long thundering ecstasy of happiness, and he will go to his death untroubled, knowing that he will soon turn up again as an author or something, and be even more intolerably capable and comfortable than ever he was before!

— *MARK TWAIN, QUOTED IN MARZLUFF & ANGELL'S*
IN THE COMPANY OF CROWS AND RAVENS

Hummingbirds

(*Selasphorus rufus and platycercus*)

According to the *Birds of New Mexico Field Guide*, there are three species of "hummers" (hummingbirds) in New Mexico. They are the black-chinned hummingbird (*Archilochus alexandri*), the broad-tailed hummingbird (*Selasphorus platycercus*), and the rufous hummingbird (*Selasphorus rufus*), and each of them is distinctive in its own right.

HUMMINGBIRD

Hikers in the mountains and foothills of New Mexico might have the good fortune of watching a black-chinned hummingbird forage at one of the hundreds of flowers it normally visits in a single day. The black-chinned hummingbird is the western counterpart of the ruby-throated hummingbird, the most wide-ranging hummer in North America. Naturalist H.G.I. Reichenbach was obviously deeply influenced by Greek mythology, as he named several hummingbird genera after Greeks—Archilochus was one of the first Greek poets. The specific epithet *alexandri* is from the name of its discoverer, a doctor who collected specimens in Mexico.

Nature's Gift to Plants

The black-chinned hummer is a rare summer breeder in the U.S. Rocky Mountains, and its habitat is riparian forests and deciduous shrubs in the foothills. The wings create a humming noise, flapping nearly 80 times per second.

The second species is the broad-tailed hummingbird. This species is a common summer breeder in the Colorado Rockies, but rare breeder in the central and northern U.S. Rockies. Its habitat is in ponderosa pine, Douglas fir, and other coniferous forests, disturbed areas, avalanche slopes, and burned areas in the montane and subalpine up to 10,000 feet. The hummer often nests over a stream in a tiny cup nest of plant down and spider webs, covered with lichen or leaves on a saddled branch.

The female incubates one to three eggs, white without markings, and will come readily to nectar feeders. Hummingbirds are the only birds with the ability to fly backward. They do not sing but will chatter or buzz to communicate, and the wingbeats produce a whistle, almost like a tiny ringing bell. The heart pumps an incredible 1,260 beats per minute.

Weighing just two to three grams, it takes about five average-sized hummers to equal the weight of a single chickadee. The male performs a spectacular pendulum-like flight over the perched female. After mating, the female builds the nest and raises the young without any help from her mate. She constructs a soft, flexible nest that expands to accommodate the growing young.

The third hummingbird that lives in New Mexico is the Rufous hummingbird. This is also a tiny (two to three grams) burnt orange-colored bird with a black throat patch (gorget) that reflects orange-red in the sunlight. It has a white chest and green-to-tan flanks. It is one of the smallest birds in the state. This is the only commonly seen copper-colored hummer in the Rockies.

This is a bold, hardy hummer. When I say bold, I mean *bold.* He chases off broad-tailed hummingbirds nearly twice his size in the blink of an eye. Kind of the "Little Big Man" of the bird world! Rufous hummingbirds live in the Western half of North America, and are long-distance migrants, with some individuals breeding in Alaska and spending the winter down in Mexico. Considering the small size of these birds, this is one of the longest migratory bird journeys of any bird in the world.

Rufous hummingbirds are known to have excellent memories, especially for location. Birds may return to the same backyard feeder year after year, pinpointing the exact location of a previously known nectar feeder. The annual migration of the hummer through the Rocky Mountains coincides with the blooming of the flowers. This hummer feeds off of (you guessed it) mostly red flowers. As with their cousins, the rufous hummingbird migrates to Central and South America.

As hummers visit flowers for food, they spread pollen from one flower to another, ensuring the plants' survival. *Don't ya just love nature!*

House Wren

(Troglodytes aedon)

HOUSE WREN

The house wren, a small plain brown bird with an effervescent voice, is a common backyard bird over nearly the entire Western hemisphere. It has a rush-and-jumble song that begins precisely at 5:18 a.m. I know because he wakes me up every morning! It beats an alarm clock any day of the week.

'The Jackson Five' of the Bird World

Small and compact with a flat head and fairly long, curved beak, this short-winged bird keeps its longish tail cocked up at a right angle to the rest of the body. Bubbly and energetic, just like their songs, look for house wrens hopping quickly through tangles and low branches and, in spring and summer, frequently pausing to deliver cheerful trilling songs. In summer, house wrens are at home in open forests, forest edges, and areas with scattered grass and trees. Backyards, farmyards, and city parks are perfect for them. The house wren, in particular, sings as though its lungs were bottomless. This strong voice was recognized by the Chippewa Indians in the northern United States, whose name for the house wren, *O-du-na-mis-sug-ud-da-we-shi*, means "big noise for its size."

Also found in Northern New Mexico, close relatives of the house wren are the rock wren, canyon wren, winter wren, marsh wren, and Bewick's wren. Each of these birds has a melodic, bubbly call that is exceptionally loud for birds so small in size. The rock wren has the most unusual habit of "paving" a walkway to their nest. They occasionally make this gravel welcome mat by carefully placing as many as 1,500 stones and pebbles, although typically only a few stones are used. The exact purpose of this paving is not clear; it might protect the nest from moisture, or it might make the nest easier to find in monotonous terrain. Rock wrens are found in canyons, cliffs, and rocky slopes throughout the West as their name implies.

The canyon wren has a lively song that is more often heard than the bird is seen. Its song echoes hauntingly through narrow canyons, cascades and ripples down melodic scales, while finishing on an unexpected up beat. These small birds forage for insects and spiders tirelessly. The sweet warbling voice of the winter wren serenades spruce-fir forests and is distinguished by its melodious, bubbly tone, and its uninterrupted song length. The length of the song alone facilitates identification because it eliminates all other forest songsters. *Troglodytes*, the scientific name for this little bird, is Greek for 'creeping in holes' or 'cave dweller,' which is a very common trait of this bird.

Next is the energetic and reclusive marsh wren. This little bird is associated with cattail marshes, wetlands, and wet meadows. Although it prefers to keep a low profile by staying hidden in deep vegetation, its distinctive song is one of the characteristic voices of our freshwater wetlands. The specific epithet for the marsh wren is *palustris*, Latin for marsh.

Last but certainly not least, the Bewick's wren is one of the hardiest of its family; it routinely overwinters through much of its range. John James Audubon chose to honor his friend Thomas Bewick in the name of this spirited songbird. Bewick was an exceptionally talented wood engraver whom Audubon visited during one of his trips to England. The long, narrow tail of the Bewick's wren waves gently from side to side as the small bird roams about. Almost mouse-like in its traveling, this wren curiously investigates all nooks and crevices of its territory.

It should be obvious that the defining characteristic for all wrens is their bubbly, melodious calls. You can't help but smile when you hear one of these feathered friends. You may wonder why I referred to wrens as "The Jackson Five" of the bird world at the outset. I did so because you've never met a more talented group of songsters.

Black-headed Grosbeak

(Pheucticus melanocephalus)

BLACK-HEADED GROSBEAK

In western North America the sweet song of the black-headed grosbeak caroling down from the treetops sounds like a tipsy robin welcoming spring, says Stan Tekiela in *Birds of New Mexico*. The flashy black, white, and cinnamon males and the less flamboyant females sing from perches in suburbs, mountain forests, and desert thickets. At feeders they effortlessly shuck sunflower seeds with their massive, heavy, two-toned gray bills.

The 'Hanz and Franz' of the Bird World

According to Cornell University's bird laboratory, the showy male black-headed grosbeak puts in equal time on the domestic front: both sexes sit on eggs, feed the young, and feistily defend their nesting territory. In flight, they flash bright yellow under the wings, and both the male and female have very large bills that are conical and thick at the base, large heads, and short thick necks. They are the Hans and Franz of the bird world! If you didn't watch *"Saturday Night Live"* in the mid-80s, you probably have no idea who I'm talking about.

Often hidden as they hop about in dense foliage gleaning insects and seeds, black-headed grosbeaks feed readily on sunflower seeds at feeders. Males sing in a rich, whistled song from treetops in spring and summer, and the short, squeaky chip note is distinctive and can be a good way to find and identify these birds. I recently watched a story on national news about a group of blind students who go out birding and identify birds by the call they make alone...very inspiring.

Look for the black-headed grosbeak in mixed woodlands and forest edges from mountain forests to thickets along desert streams, to backyards and gardens. Ideal habitat includes some large trees and a diverse understory. Just look for a stocky bird, burnt orange in color, and an unusually large two-toned bill (dark upper bill, lighter lower bill). Overall, the bird is actually increasing in numbers in New Mexico and the United States.

Dusky Blue Grouse

(Dendragapus obscurus)

DUSKY BLUE GROUSE

Fall is a special time of year to be in the high mountains of Taos County and the western US. The days are cool, nights are crisp, and all is really right with the world. Taxonomists have identified two species of the blue grouse: the sooty blue grouse and the dusky blue grouse, with multiple subspecies of each (seven to be exact). For our purposes here we will deal only with the dusky blue grouse, which is found in the four corners states plus Nevada and south-central Wyoming.

The higher elevations of Northern New Mexico and also the mountain ranges in the southern and southwestern part of the state have viable populations of dusky blue grouse. Blue grouse are birds of the high mountain country, typically vegetated with aspen, Douglas-fir and Engelmann spruce. Locating blue grouse below 8,500-feet elevation is uncommon. On several occasions I have encountered them at or even above timberline.

Blue grouse do not typically range too far from dense stands of cover provided by the previously mentioned conifers, aspen, currants (ribes), wild raspberries and other ground shrubs. In *Game Birds of North America*, Leonard Lee Rue III advises us to look for seeps, springs, and other water sources that tend to hold green forbs and a variety of insects later into the fall. I have frequently encountered blue grouse on abandoned logging roads and the adjacent forest or feeding in meadow clearings within dense conifer cover. The pursuit of these 'blues' is certainly no walk in the park. It seems to me that I spend more time hoofing it uphill as opposed to semi-level or downhill slopes.

Blue grouse utilize a wide variety of food sources. Early in the year the hen and her brood will feed heavily on insects, particularly grasshoppers, but also ants and beetles. Currants, elderberries, raspberries, vetch, strawberries, aspen leaves, dandelions, clover blooms and buds comprise the majority of their fall diet. As fall progresses, the birds will become dependent on available plant sources and ultimately, as fall wanes, the birds will feed almost exclusively on the needles and buds of Douglas fir and other conifers. This is their feeding practice until the next spring.

Blue grouse are not very vocal except during the breeding season; anyone who has heard the males' "booming" as it is sometimes called, remarks on its ventriloquistic qualities. Some say it sounds like a growling or groaning.

The adult male blue grouse is about 20 to 22 inches in length, has a wingspan of about 28 inches and weighs up to 3.5 pounds. The male is grayish-brown with a white throat and dark slate-black tail with a gray terminal band, while the female is more brown than gray. The bird's throat, face, breast and belly are a slate-toned blue-gray; there is a white line running through the eye and bright yellow comb above the eye. Hidden by the feathers on each side of the neck are golf-ball sized orange air sacs. The sacs and feathers look exactly like a fried egg.

The blue grouse is capable of flying at speeds of 25 mph, which is usually more than sufficient for the bird to disappear quickly behind intervening trees. The short, cupped wings of the blue grouse allow it a rapid takeoff, and after reaching its top speed, it soars for as long a distance as it needs before landing.

The blue grouse does not migrate south like other birds. And curiously enough, whereas all the creatures of the western mountains descend to lower elevations as the temperatures drop and the snow depths increase, the blue grouse works its way higher up into the mountains. Here, the birds will congregate in the tops of huge fir trees, which provide them with both food and shelter. Again: *Don't ya just love nature!*

Hermit Thrush

(Catharus guttatus)

I remember when we lived near the entrance of Lostine Canyon in northeast Oregon, Diane and I would go for a walk late in the evening with my Siberian husky Sierra, and we'd come across the bird with the "flute-like call." Never did see the bird, but the call it made was unmistakable.

HERMIT THRUSH

The Bird Call of Bird Calls

Chris Fisher, author of *Birds of the Rocky Mountains,* informs us that beauty in forest birds is often gauged by sound and not appearance. Given this criterion, the hermit thrush is certainly one of the most beautiful birds to inhabit Rocky Mountain forests. This unassuming bird with a lovely melancholy song lurks in the understories of far Northern forests in the summer and is a frequent winter companion across much of the country, including New Mexico in the winter. In Taos County we are very fortunate to catch a glimpse of this bird for a very short time in spring while it is making its way back to its breeding grounds up north.

The hermit thrush forages on the forest floor by rummaging through leaf litter or seizing insects with its bill. The hermit thrush has a rich, brown upper body with smudged spots on its breast, with a reddish tail that sets it apart from similar species in its genus. Fisher says that the bird's red tail "reminds one of a lonely old hermit wearing nothing but a pair of red long underwear."

The scientific name *guttatus* is Latin for 'spotted' or 'speckled,' in reference to the breast of the bird. Another distinguishing trait is the pale white-eye ring. This bird prefers spruce-fir forests, avalanche slopes, and lodgepole pine forests in the upper montane of the subalpine eco-zone. In other words, the bird likes the high country.

Many features of the hermit thrush can be remembered by association with its name. Its memorable song always begins with a single, high, lone note, always ascending in tone in an upward spiral. The hermit thrush nests in a small trees or shrubs, in a cup-like nest built with grass, twigs and mud; the female incubates four eggs for up to 13 days. The hermit thrush is similar in appearance to the Swainson's thrush and the fox sparrow.

Great Horned Owl

(*Bubo virginianus*)

GREAT HORNED OWL

The great horned owl, also known as the tiger owl, is a very adaptable bird with a vast range and is the most widely distributed true owl in the Americas. The great horned owl is the second heaviest owl in North America, second only to the closely related but very different looking snowy owl (*B. scandiacus*).

The length of the great horned owl is 17 to 25 inches with a wingspan of 36 to 60 inches. It weighs about 3.1 pounds, although it looks much heavier (feathers just make them look heavy). Females are invariably somewhat larger than males, as is common in nature. There is considerable variation in plumage coloration but not in body shape. This is a heavily built, barrel-shaped species that has a large head and very broad wings, with a prominent facial disk that is reddish-brown or gray in color. There is also a white patch on its throat.

The iris of the eye is yellow, and its "horns" are neither ears nor horns, simply tufts of feathers that give them a very distinctive look. It is the only very large owl in its range to have them.

The legs and feet are covered in feathers up to the talons, with some black skin peeking out from around the talons. The feet and talons are distinctively large and powerful. Other Bubo owl species have comparable and formidable feet. Its call is a low-pitched but loud *ho-ho-hoo hoo hoo*; sometimes it is only four syllables instead of five. The female's call is higher and rises in pitch at the end of the call, much like that of a Mexican spotted owl's four-note hoot.

There are 13 subspecies of the great horned owl, and like most owls, it makes great use of secrecy and stealth. Due to its natural-colored plumage, it is well camouflaged both while active at night and roosting during the day. Despite this, it can still sometimes be spotted in its daytime roosts, which are typically large conifer trees or on rocks. This regularly leads to them being 'mobbed' by other birds, especially American crows.

The Opportunistic Hunter

Owls have spectacular binocular vision, allowing them to pinpoint prey and see in low light. The eyes of a great horned owl are nearly as large as those of a human being and are immobile in their eye sockets. As a result, instead of turning its eyes, an owl must turn its whole head, the neck capable of rotating a full 270 degrees in order to see in various directions without moving its entire body.

An owl's hearing is as good as, if not better than, its vision. Owls have much better depth perception and better perception of sound elevation (up-down direction) than human beings. This is due to the owl's ears not being located in the same position on both sides of the head. The right ear is typically set higher in the skull and at a slightly different angle. By tilting or turning its head until the sound is the same in both ears, an owl can pinpoint both the horizontal and vertical direction of the sound's source.

This explains how a great horned owl could swoop down and snatch a field mouse from underneath a foot of snow without ever seeing it in "*Marty Stouffer's Wild America*." Prey can vary greatly based on opportunity. It has been said that nearly any living creature can be the great horned owl's legitimate prey! *Ain't nature grand!*

Flammulated Owl

(*Otus flammeolus*)

FLAMMULATED OWL

I first met this little bird in 1992, thanks to a friendship with Dr. Brian Linkhart, while working on the Manitou Experimental Forest in central Colorado. A flammulated owl researcher for over two decades and an Associate Professor at Colorado College, Brian's passion was to document the ecology of this small owl.

It was once known as a Forest Service 'sensitive' species, one step away from being listed as a federally threatened or endangered species. Much has since been learned about this small, secretive owl, and in most of its range, including the Carson National Forest, it is no longer considered a sensitive species. This is due in large part to the work of Dr. Linkhart and other scientists.

The Ghost in the Darkness

The flammulated owl is a small, nocturnal owl approximately 6 inches long with a 14-inch wingspan. *Flammuleous* is the Latin root word for flammulated. It describes the flame-like markings on its face and wings. It is the only small owl in its range that has dark eyes, a telltale symbol of the species.

This small owl has a rather wide but patchy distribution in the mountains of the western United States. Its breeding range extends from southern British Columbia to northern Mexico. Flammulated owls are migratory and winter from Mexico south to Guatemala. Its secretive nature and widely scattered distribution make it very difficult to gauge population trends for this species. A bird of the mountain forests, it apparently prefers areas with old ponderosa pine intermixed with Gambel oak, aspen, Douglas fir, and shrubby undergrowth. An insect eater, this small owl grabs prey from leaves with its talons while hovering.

Nests are in tree cavities excavated by woodpeckers; the owls are sometimes known to use nest boxes. The female lays two to three eggs, and the owlets are fed by the male at an average rate of seven or eight prey per hour. Their primary prey items are moths, particularly those known as miller moths, which are numerous in the early spring.

In 2007, Dr. Linkhart and his crew documented the first observed instance of polygyny in flammulated owls. Polygyny is one male owl with two breeding female owls. The two nests were separated by two weeks, and each nest initially consisted of three owlets. The male delivered considerably less prey to the secondary nest. Evidence suggested that all owlets fledged from the primary nest but only one of three fledged from the secondary nest. The scientists were uncertain of the cause of polygyny, but suspect that the Hayman wildfire, the largest wildfire in Colorado's history, may have played a role.

To date, there has been little effort to manage for this species. Further study is needed regarding the bird's specific habitat needs before management policies can be created. Most researchers believe the biggest human-induced threat to be from logging. Flammulated owls have one of the slowest reproductive rates of North American owls, and we need a much better understanding of the breeding biology of these small owls.

Evening Grosbeak

(*Coccothraustes vespertinus*)

Taos is located at the southern tip of this bird's year-round range, but evening grosbeak are commonly seen in winter in Taos County. They are known as an "irruptive" species, meaning that their population size and range is not fixed, but moves around in search of food.

EVENING GROSBEAK

The evening grosbeaks' breeding habitat is coniferous and mixed forest across Canada and the western mountainous areas of the U.S. and Mexico. The range of this bird has expanded far to the east in historical times, possibly due to plantings of maples and shrubs around farms and the wide availability of bird feeders in winter. A large flock of evening grosbeaks' with a hearty appetite can quickly wipe out a birdfeeder!

An Irruptive Species

But what exactly is an irruption? An irruption is a dramatic, irregular migration of large numbers of birds to areas where they aren't typically found, possibly at a great distance from their normal range. The spruce budworm outbreak throughout Northern New Mexico in the late 1980s created an irruption of evening grosbeaks and other birds, as they came to take advantage of a plentiful food source. Other birds that irrupt include pine siskins, pine grosbeaks, red crossbills, among others.

The evening grosbeak is a type of finch, and as a result, they have a plump and sturdy body. The most obvious feature of the evening grosbeak is definitely their bright colors. Apparently, the male doesn't have any confidence issues with his bright yellow feathers that are complemented nicely by his black tail and wing feathers. To complete the ensemble the males have a nice white shoulder patch. The females, on the other hand, have a silver-gray body with pale yellow sides and rump. Like most birds, the females are not as flashy as their male companions.

Before we continue, I want you to think about how you eat sunflower seeds. You know those Ranch- or salt-flavored seeds that are perfect for entertaining? Have you pictured yourself happily chomping away on these seeds? Now it is time to learn how a professional sunflower seedeater does it. The evening grosbeak will carefully roll the sunflower seed over and over in their mouth until it is sitting perfectly along the sharp edge of their beak. Once they are happy with the position they will slice through the shell with their beak and eat the prize inside. At this point the shell gets discarded, and the bird is ready for round two. I guess it really isn't much different than how we do it. I had just assumed they ate the shell and all, like I did when I was a kid.

I'm sure Native Americans were aware of evening grosbeaks before any record was made of them in written English. Indeed, the Ojibwe Indian name for them—as transcribed by Henry Schoolcraft in 1823—was '*paushkundamo*'. This is derived from their word for breaking something such as a berry, referring to the grosbeak's style of eating. Schoolcraft also provided the first record ornithologists have of the species. Whatever their origins, we are fortunate to host them for a short time most winters.

Common Goldeneye

(*Bucephala clangula*)

COMMON GOLDENEYE

For those of you who have driven to Santa Fe lately, you have no doubt seen the little black-and-white duck floating on the Rio Grande River and wondered, "Hey, what is that handsome little black-and-white duck?" Well, I'm here to tell you everything you wanted to know about the common goldeneye but were afraid to ask.

Called a 'diver' duck, as opposed to a 'dabbler'—which you have with the mallard and Cinnamon teal—the divers like to feed on the bottom on aquatic plants and insects. They are particularly partial to mollusks. The common goldeneye is also referred to as a 'whistler' because of the loud sound produced by the wings. This identifies them even at night when they fly overhead to get from one feeding ground to another. The whistler has always reminded me of a duck going to prom, dressed up all fancy-like in his black-and-white tuxedo.

The common goldeneye breeds throughout Canada and Alaska, in the northern states of Montana, Wyoming, North Dakota and Minnesota. They can be seen in late winter in the southern states including New Mexico, before they make their return trip to their breeding grounds.

The Little Duck Wearing a Tux

During courtship display, which begins in late winter, the male stretches his head forward along the water, and then throws his head back rapidly upward and over his back, his bill pointed skyward, while uttering a loud rasping note. Then he swings his orange feet forward, sending up a spray of water in front of his own bad self. Such drama!

The male goldeneye has a white body, black-appearing head (actually it's glossy, dark-greenish), and a large round white eyespot in front of a bright yellow eye. This is the defining feature of this handsome little duck.

Cinnamon Teal

(*Anas cyanoptera*)

CINNAMON TEAL

The morning sun strikes the waters of the Rio Grande River, and one of the most beautiful ducks I have ever seen, the male cinnamon teal, glows on the backwaters like embers from a fire. These handsome ducks are frequently seen swimming along the water's surface, their heads partially submerged, skimming aquatic life from the water's surface.

Often a series of ducks can be seen following a lead foraging individual, taking advantage of the sediments the lead duck stirs up with its paddling feet. The scientific name—from *cyano* meaning blue, and *ptera* meaning wing—the cinnamon teal's name reinforces the similarities of this species to its primo, the blue-winged teal, with which it has been known to interbreed.

In *Birds of the Rocky Mountains*, Fisher informs us that the female cinnamon teal have been known to put on a 'broken wing' act to distract predators from their ducklings. We learn that the male cinnamon teal, unlike most male ducks, often stays with his mate through most of the incubation; sometimes the male has even been seen accompanying his mate and her brood.

Red Eye, Not a Hangover!

Like blue-winged teal, the cinnamon teal has a long, broad bill and a blue forewing patch with an iridescent green wing patch called a speculum behind it. Perhaps their most unique characteristic is the red eyes, that and the rich cinnamon-red head, neck, breast and belly. They are a common summer breeder in the southern and central

U.S. Rockies. They nest in tall vegetation, typically far from water—a quarter mile or so, in a well-concealed hollow built with grass and down. The females incubate seven to 12 eggs for 21 to 25 days, and the ducklings fly after seven weeks. The male has a *whistled peep* while the female has a rough *karr, karr, karr.*

I remember well seeing my first male cinnamon teal with a group of mallards while counting double-crested cormorants in a wetland on the Imperial National Wildlife Refuge in Arizona. I was in a canoe at the time. I remember saying to myself, "I sure chose the right profession." I know it's cliché, but do what you love, and you'll never work a day in your life! It's true!

Cassin's Finch

(*Carpodacus cassinii*)

CASSIN'S FINCH

In some parts of the Rocky Mountains, Cassin's finch are the most common birds but only for a few short days before they move to higher elevations during the breeding season. Their mass migration frequently brings them down to town-sites for a short time, says Chris Fisher in *Birds of the Rocky Mountains.*

This must be what I experienced. One day the bird is hanging out in the front yard, and the next he is nowhere to be found. Once the birds have moved on, they are more difficult to see, but their bubbling courtship song serves as a pleasant reminder of their time in town. John Cassin, from whom the bird gets its name, was one of the leading 19th century taxonomists whose name graces four different bird species.

The male of the species has a reddish crown, throat and rump, mottled brown under-parts, and a deeply notched tail. As typical, the female is indistinct. In summer it frequents spruce-fir and sub-alpine fir forests, and migrates to pinyon-juniper, Douglas fir and ponderosa pine forests of the montane zone in the winter. The Cassin's finch eats mostly seeds, but also eats insects and buds in spring and berries in winter. The bird is a regular visitor to birdfeeders.

The Cassin's finch nests in coniferous forests of lodgepole pine, ponderosa pine and Douglas fir, and are typically found at high altitudes (10,000 to 11,000 feet). The birds nest in colonies or singly, almost always in large conifers, usually 15 to 60 feet above the ground. The average is 30 feet above ground.

According to *Peterson's Field Guide to Western Bird Nests*, the female lays three to six oval, slightly glossy eggs that are bluish-green and speckled with brown or black. The female incubates for 12 or more days, with the possibility of two broods in one season.

Birds of North America (National Geographic) states that the red hues of the Cassin's finch begin to appear later in the summer, and I've seen pictures where the color variation, depending on the season, would make you think it is not a Cassin's finch you are looking at. I don't worry too much about it—I've only been wrong twice in my life...I can afford to give one up! Just kidding!

National Geographic explains topography as creating a mental map of each bird by dividing its body into separate areas. Field guides usually contain a diagram labeling the different parts of a bird's body. By consulting the diagram and the field guides text on purple and Cassin's finches, a bird watcher will learn that the back is reddish in a male purple finch but brownish in a male Cassin's finch.

A birder will also learn that the head pattern of eyebrow, cheek, and mustache is more prominent in the female purple finch than in the female Cassin's finch. Such are the keys to sorting out similar species—clearly not a skill easily mastered. But for anyone who has sampled the pleasures of bird watching, becoming familiar with their topography is an essential step toward *seeing* the birds more knowledgeably, and thus enjoying them more.

Western Bluebird

(*Sialia curricoides*)

WESTERN BLUERBIRD

When I say bluebirds, you would be correct in asking if I am referring to the western bluebird (*Sialia mexicana*), the mountain bluebird (*Sialia currucoides*), or the eastern bluebird (*Sialia sialis*). All three species can be found in New Mexico. Both the western and mountain bluebirds nest in the state with populations of both species increasing in the winter as birds from further north migrate into the state for the winter. An isolated resident population of eastern bluebirds can be found in the very southwest corner of the state. Eastern bluebirds also migrate into the eastern half of the state in the winter.

Blue as the New Mexico Skies

The bluebird is well named, for it wears a coat of the purest, richest, most gorgeous blue on its back, wings, and tail; no other North American bird better deserves the name, for no other flashes before our admiring eyes so much brilliant blue. It has been said that he carries on his back the blue of heaven and the rich brown of freshly turned earth on his breast (at least in the case of the western bluebird), but who has ever seen the bluest sky as blue as the bluebird's back? I came across that description of the eastern bluebird in the great ornithologist Arthur Cleveland Bent's series of books on North American birds.

Bluebirds are usually found in fields, open woodlands, parks or along golf courses or other open areas, including suburban locations with open spaces and scattered trees of the American West. In the case of the western bluebird, brilliant blue-and-rust colored bluebirds sit on low perches and swoop lightly to the ground to catch insects. Deep blue, rusty, and white, males are considerably brighter than the gray-brown, blue-tinged females.

In the mountains, they are found in clearings and meadows. The mountain bluebird is well-known for its hovering flight as it 'hawks' for insects. This bird was one of my fondest memories of living at the Manitou Experimental Forest near Woodland Park, Colorado. My good friend Diane always admired how the male would feed the female as she sat on the nest, and was impressed with how they could build a nest while entering such a small hole.

This small thrush nests in holes in trees or nest boxes and often gathers in small flocks to feed on insects or berries, giving their quiet, chortling calls. The eastern bluebird has a musical flight call that often reveals its presence.

Bluebirds can be attracted to peanut butter mixes, suet and fruit. Raisins soaked in hot water to soften them are well received, as are mealworms (a special favorite of the bluebird). If you manage a bluebird house, watch for house sparrows trying to use the nest box and immediately remove any house sparrow nesting material. All three species of bluebirds nest in New Mexico, although the nesting range of the eastern bluebird is very limited. One, two and sometimes three broods of four to six chicks may be raised. Eggs are pale blue or rarely white.

From *Pueblo Birds & Myths*, by Hamilton Tyler, I learned there are separate names in most Pueblo languages for the western and the mountain bluebird, and at Zuni Pueblo the ceremonial usage of the two species seems to be distinct. Both are winter birds because they descend to the lowlands along with the snow and the cold of that season. But they also make their way back toward the mountains in the spring with the intent of breeding at higher elevations. In spring they flock together in local migrations and are thus more visible. The passage of large numbers in spring and again in the fall makes them excellent symbols of transition between the seasons.

Canada Goose

(Branta Canadensis)

CANADA GOOSE

The Canada goose is native to North America, including New Mexico. It breeds in Canada and the northern United States in a variety of habitats. Its nest is usually located in an elevated area near water such as streams, rivers, lakes, and ponds, as well as sometimes on a beaver lodge. Its eggs are laid in a shallow depression lined with plant material and down.

The male goose, called a gander, can be very aggressive in defending its territory. The female goose looks virtually identical but is generally ten 10 percent smaller than its male counterpart and has a different honk. The black head and neck with white chinstraps distinguish the Canada goose from all other goose species. The life span of geese in the wild is 10-24 years.

By the early 20th century, over-hunting and loss of habitat resulted in a serious decline in the numbers of this bird in its native range. The Giant Canada Goose subspecies was believed to be extinct in the 1950s until, in 1962, a small flock was discovered wintering in Rochester, Minnesota. With improved game laws and habitat re-creation and preservation programs, their populations have recovered in most of their range.

In recent years, Canada goose populations in some areas have grown substantially, so much so that many consider them to be pests for their droppings, the bacteria in their droppings, noise, and confrontational behavior. Who can forget the recent airplane crashes attributed to collisions with flocks of geese?

Like most geese, the Canada goose is naturally migratory. The calls overhead from large groups of Canada geese flying in V-shaped formation signal the transitions into spring and autumn.

Contrary to their normal migration routine, some flocks never migrate, even during the winter, where food is available throughout the year. They have become "resident" birds. Such is the case with the geese that occupy the upper Río Grande near Wild Rivers, the Río Grande River near Pilar, and the Río Chama.

Canada geese are primarily herbivores. Their diet consists of green vegetation and grains. In the water, they feed from silt at the bottom of the body of water. The goose also feeds on aquatic plants, such as seaweed and duckweed, and occasionally on small insects and fish.

What's Good for the Goose Is Good for the Gander

During the second year of their lives, Canada geese find a mate. They are monogamous, and most couples stay together all of their lives. If one dies, the other may find a new mate. Females lay three to eight eggs and both parents protect the nest while the eggs incubate, but the female spends more time at the nest than the male. Known egg predators include coyotes, foxes, raccoons, common raven, American crows and bears.

The incubation period, in which the female incubates while the male remains nearby, lasts for 24-28 days after the eggs are laid. As the annual summer molt also takes place during the breeding season, the adults lose their flight feathers for 20-40 days, regaining flight at about the same time as their goslings start to fly.

Adult geese are often seen leading their goslings in a line, usually with one parent at the front, and the other at the back. While protecting their goslings, parents often violently chase away nearby creatures, from small birds to humans that approach, after warning them by giving off a hissing sound. Although parents are hostile to unfamiliar geese, they may form groups of a number of goslings and a few adults known as "crèches."

Great Blue Heron

(Ardea Herodias)

According to *Birds of the Rocky Mountains* by Chris Fisher, the great blue heron is the patient sentry of wetland marshes. It stands motionless as it surveys the calm, shallow waters, head-and-shoulders above most other wetland birds waiting for a small fish, amphibian, reptile, small mammal, or aquatic invertebrate to wander by. Being a predator in the wild is not an easy life, and patience is your most valuable asset.

GREAT BLUE HERON

Patient Sentry of the Marsh

I used to sit and watch the great blue herons on the marsh at Sherburne National Wildlife Refuge in central Minnesota. It was my first job as a refuge manager on a cooperative education work phase with the U.S. Fish and Wildlife Service. It was then that I first knew I had chosen the right profession. I learned to stay patient, to "keep my eyes on the prize," and to never give up on my dreams. These are important lessons for those just starting out in life.

OK, enough preaching. This heron is often mistaken for the sandhill crane because of its similar size, but cranes hold their necks outstretched in flight whereas herons and egrets fold their necks back on their shoulders—a specialized vertebra enables herons to contort their necks into an S-shape. Occasionally, people out fishing will catch a large trout that has distinctive triangular scars, which is evidence that the fish has survived a close encounter with a heron.

The great blue heron is usually quiet, but occasionally gives a deep, harsh *frahnk, frahnk, frahnk*, usually during takeoff. The heron is frequently encountered along the edges of rivers through most of the

Rocky Mountains, and can be seen locally along the banks of the Rio Grande near Pilar, at Taos Junction, and Wild Rivers near Questa. According to Fisher's guidebook, the great blue heron is a colonial nester in large trees. The nest is a flimsy to elaborate stick and twig platform that is added to over the years, and can be up to 4 feet in diameter. *Ain't nature grand!*

Fisher describes this colonial nester as a large, blue-gray bird with a long curving neck, long dark legs, chestnut-colored thighs and a pointed yellow bill. According to *Birding*, a Nature Company Guide, the great blue heron is unmistakable throughout most of its range. The exception is in the Florida Keys where you may find an all-white form of this bird, once considered a separate species.

Black-crowned Night Heron

(Nycticorax nycticorax)

BLACK-CROWNED NIGHT HERON

It is a special treat to see these birds because they are "crepuscular," meaning they are most active at night or dusk when the only thing you may see is their ghostly forms flapping out from daytime roosts to feed in wetlands. You are more likely to hear the squawking of the bird as it patrols the wetlands adjacent to rivers and creeks. Stan Tekiela describes the black-crowned night heron in *Birds of New Mexico* as a stocky, hunched-over, inactive bird when compared to their long-legged and long-necked heron relatives, the great blue heron. Sterry and Small in *Birds of Western North America* give perhaps the most memorable description of the bird: "stocky heron with proportionately large head and hunchbacked appearance at rest."

Inventor of Night Fishing

In the light of day, the adults have strikingly gray-and-black feathers on the back, gray wings, long white head plumes with a white belly, and red eyes. Cornell University's *All About Birds* says these social birds breed in colonies of stick nests usually over or very near water and are the most widespread heron in the world. The long white head plumes and red eyes are perhaps the most memorable things about the bird, like the black-crowned night heron is just coming back from the beautician's after a late night at the club. *OK, OK, I have a very lively imagination!*

One memory that I have of the black-crowned night heron comes from conducting waterfowl surveys via canoe in a wetland in central

Minnesota in the early 80s. I heard the squawking of the heron while it was still dark—it scared the bajeebers out of me! I had no idea what it was at the time. Even now that I do know, it is still a treat to hear one, let alone see one.

I would like to close with an excerpt from Chris C. Fisher's *Birds of the Rocky Mountains*:

> When the setting sun's dim light has driven most of the wetland's waders to their nightly roosts, the black-crowned night heron arrives to reawaken these feeding areas with its characteristic squawk. A night heron's eyes are proportionately larger than other herons'—likely an adaptation to foraging in low light. Most of the night herons that migrate through low passes in the Rockies have over-wintered in California and are destined to breed on the Great Plains. This heron's white "ponytail" is present for most of the year, but it is most noticeable during the breeding season. Nycticorax, meaning 'night raven,' refers to this bird's characteristic nighttime call.

White-tailed Ptarmigan

(Lagopus leucura)

WHITE-TAILED PTARMIGAN

The smallest grouse in North America, the white-tailed ptarmigan inhabits alpine habitat from Alaska to New Mexico. In the latter, it is found near the summit of Wheeler Peak and in the Pecos Wilderness area.

It has numerous adaptations to its severe habitat, including feathered toes, highly cryptic coloration, and an energy-conserving daily regimen. Found only above timberline, typically above 12,000 feet, the white-tailed ptarmigan leads a very sedentary lifestyle in winter to conserve precious energy by avoiding flight and often roosting in snow banks. Warm weather may stress the white-tailed ptarmigan, and it can be seen bathing in snow when the temperature is higher than 70 degrees Fahrenheit.

Master of Habitat Adaptation

Buds, stems and seeds make up the majority of its diet in the winter, along with insects, leaves, fruits and flowers in the summer months. Females nest on a scrape on the ground, with some vegetation pulled by the female around her body to form a rim. The clutch size is between two and eight eggs. Eggs are light cinnamon in color, showing dark spots toward the time of hatching.

The chicks are completely covered with dense down, eyes open, and leave the nest within six to twelve hours after the last egg hatches. This means they are considered precocial or precocious in displaying adult qualities at a very early age, and as opposed to altricial, which describe species that require care and feeding by adults for a period of time.

Strutting before the female, the male bird bows and with its red eye combs flared and its tail fanned out, walks on the ground nipping at vegetation—clucking to himself: "That's right, I'm bad!" He consumes grit (gravel) to aid in processing the plant material—making his own bad self even badder by eating a mouthful of rocks.

The white-tailed ptarmigan goes through a molting known as 'cryptic coloration' with the change of seasons, changing feathers from pure white in the winter months to streaked brown and gray feathers in summer. The tail feathers remain white throughout the year. This change in color allows them to blend in with their surroundings exceptionally well, as the photograph clearly demonstrates.

Some disturbances, including ski area development, over-grazing, and excessive hiking trails, may negatively affect the distribution of white-tailed ptarmigan on a local scale.

American Robin

(Turdus migratorius)

AMERICAN ROBIN

The robin seems to be a bird perfectly designed for human awareness: a classic bird, builder of classic bird nests, classic colorful plumage. Most Americans, I suspect, can identify a robin. Robins hop along in easy view of humans throughout North America. They are at home on the tundra, at 12,000-foot elevations in the Rocky Mountains, along small streams and large rivers of the Sangre de Cristo mountains, and of course, in your own backyard lawn.

I have reached hurriedly for my binoculars to identify a passing bird and have been disappointed to find it was just a robin. In the words of Joan Dunning in *Secrets of the Nest*: "I have since made a conscious effort to avoid taking robins for granted. I simply have to remember that they belong to the 'Thrush family' of birds… among the most beautiful and talented 'songsters' in the bird world."

I once described the hermit thrush as "this unassuming bird with a lovely melancholy song and a flute-like call." The same can be said of the American robin. Actually, robins were not always so common, but benefitted from the settling of North America. Robins are not adapted to deep forests, and even the Great Plains of the Midwest were too dry and scarce of earthworms to support robins.

But settlers moved west, clutching axes, irrigation pipe, and potted plants hosting earthworms for their future gardens. Things got even better with the spread of the suburbs, as the robin is happiest in that ultimate civilized setting: a nice neighborhood of little houses surrounded by trimmed lawns and shade trees with a golf course or park nearby. In such a setting there is little reason for conflict between robins and humans, and while robins that breed in remote areas are generally shy of people, the suburban robin boldly hops by in plain view, building a nest that is one of the most easily recognized of any bird.

It is the spring if you see robins; they are most likely nesting or about to nest. Robins are among the first birds to arrive on their breeding grounds, the males preceding the females by a few days. With the arrival of spring, flocks of males can be seen heading north from their wintering grounds, dispersing as the birds near their natal areas (where they were born), often returning to the exact territories in which they nested the year before.

One can tell a male robin from a female by his more intense red breast and darker brown head and tail. These colors, set against the bright green of a lawn, are the classic stuff of kids' paintings. As the ground warms in the spring, earthworms move up from below and when they begin to emerge, robins pull them out of the ground. Contrary to what I was taught in elementary school, a robin standing on the grass cocking his head sideways is not listening for worms but watching for them. He cocks his head because his eyes are on the sides of his head not directly in front. *Ain't nature grand!*

Robin-egg Blue: A Classic Color

Two days after nest construction is complete, one sky blue egg is visible in the bowl of the nest. Members of the thrush family lay some of the most beautiful of all bird eggs, and nearly everyone is familiar with the color called robin-egg blue. The eggshell is a rich blue-green lying on the muted yellow-green of the fine grass. Each morning there is another egg, but not until the clutch of four is complete does the female robin stay on the nest and begin incubation. Thus, all of the nestlings will hatch within 24 hours of each other.

The male and female robins are always close by and immediately return to the nest if danger threatens. Several times each day the female robin hops on the rim of her nest and with her beak, turns each of the eggs, so that the yolk inside will not adhere to the inside of the shell.

Joan Dunning wrote in *Secrets of the Nest*, "There is probably no baby bird so pathetically helpless as a newly hatched robin." Altricial hatchlings are among the ugliest infants in the animal kingdom, with their naked, bright pink skin; grotesquely huge black eyes only visible through closed, translucent lids; long, skinny necks; and disproportionately large, swollen stomachs. I'm telling you, it's a baby only a mother could love!

Cliff Swallow

(Petrochelidon pyrrhonota)

CLIFF SWALLOW

A uniquely patterned swallow with a dark back, wings and cap, with distinctive tan-to-rust rump, cheeks and forehead, this small bird is a master craftsman of mud nests. They are common around bridges, especially bridges over water, and rural housing (especially in open country close to cliffs). Cliff swallows construct a gourd-shaped nest out of mud with a funnel-like entrance pointing down. This bird is a colony nester with many nests lined up beneath eaves of buildings or under cliff overhangs. A cliff swallow will carry balls of mud up to 1 mile to construct its nest, according to Stan Tekiela, author of *Birds of New Mexico.*

The Master Craftsman

Many individuals in the colony return to the same nest sites each year. I can testify to this, as cliff swallows built their nests on the light fixtures in the porch of Manitou Experimental Forest where I worked in central Colorado for 17 years. It is not unusual for cliff swallows to have two broods in one season. If the number of nests beneath eaves becomes a problem, wait until after the young have left the nests to hose off the mud.

The famed "Swallows of Capistrano," the cliff swallow is the bird whose faithful return to the adobe walls of that California Mission is the cause for an annual celebration. I had heard a nasty rumor that the swallows of Capistrano had left and taken up residence on a nearby creek. But I wouldn't believe such a nasty rumor unless I saw it for myself!

I checked it out, and it turns out the cliff swallows *still* return to San Juan Capistrano Mission on or about March 19 of every year on their return trip from their wintering grounds in Argentina, and visitors from all parts of the world and all walks of life gather in great numbers to witness "the return of the swallows." They also now frequent the Chino Hills in California to the north of the village of San Juan Capistrano. *Ah, life is as it should be!*

Homeowners in the Ranchitos area of Taos who have hosted nesting swallows for three years were telling me that last year the birds were about six weeks early, arriving in early May. June 20 is their normal arrival date for this area.

There are actually three other species of swallow that live in New Mexico, including Taos County. They are the barn swallow, the tree swallow, and the violet-green swallow. Each is common in its own right, and is equally beautiful in plumage-color. All four species are talented insect-eaters! According to Sterry and Small in *Birds of Western North America*, there are seven species of swallow in Western North America in all.

DE LA TIERRA

Mammals

Short-tailed Weasel

(Mustela erminea)

SHORT-TAILED WEASEL

Weasels have an image problem: they are often described as little pointy-nosed villains and are frequently used to characterize dishonest cheats according to Pattie, Fisher and Hartson in *Mammals of the Rocky Mountains* (2000). These representations are unjust, however, because weasels are not manipulators, but rather earnest and efficient little predators.

Cute, but a Predator Extraordinaire

The short-tailed weasel is the Rocky Mountains' most common weasel, and it may be the most abundant land carnivore. Despite its abundance, the short-tailed weasel is not commonly seen, because, like all weasels, it tends to be most active at night and lives in areas with heavy cover. As short-tailed weasels roam about their ranges, they explore every hole in the ground, burrow, hollow log or brush pile for potential prey, which consists almost entirely of small mammals like mice, voles, shrews, chipmunks, pocket gophers, pikas, rabbits, bird eggs and nestlings, insects and even amphibians. Short-tailed weasels commonly take over the burrows and nests of their prey and modify them for their own use. That's like adding insult to injury! Weasels are quick and unrelenting in their pursuit of anything they can overpower.

The short summer coat of the weasel has brown upperparts and creamy white underparts, often suffused with lemon yellow. Weasels have black beady eyes that glow bright emerald green when caught in headlights at night; they have a black-tipped tail, short oval ears that extend noticeably above their elongated head, and a long neck and narrow thorax that gives them a snake-like appearance. According to Pattie, Fisher and Hartson in *Mammals of the Rocky Mountains* (2000), starting in October and November these animals become completely white, except for the black-tipped tail, and in late March or April the weasel molts back to its brown summer coat. *Ain't nature grand!* The short-tailed weasel has well-developed scent glands which produce a strong musky odor. Unlike skunks, which spray their musk, the short-tailed weasel drags and rubs its body over surfaces in order to leave its scent. *Kinda' like the way my Siberian husky Sierra used to do with dead animals!*

The short-tailed weasel's dramatic change between its white winter and brown summer coat led Europeans to give it two different names: an animal wearing the brown summer coat is called a "stoat" and in its white winter pelage it is known as an "ermine."

There was a picture of the white-phase of the short-tailed weasel standing on top of a wood pile stacked with orange-colored larch trees against a background of a blanket of fresh snow at a gallery in Jackson Hole, Wyoming. I didn't buy it...a missed opportunity!

The short-tailed weasel mates in July - August with "implantation" of the fertilized egg on the uterine wall being delayed until about March of the following year. This delayed implantation ensures survival of the kits until their food source is readily available. The weasel gives birth to four to 12 blind, helpless kits, otherwise known as altricial, that weigh just 1/16 of an ounce, open their eyes at five weeks of age, and soon thereafter accompany the adults on hunting excursions.

American Marten

(Martes Americana)

AMERICAN MARTEN

Ferocity and playfulness are perfectly blended in this quick, active, agile weasel that is equally at home on the forest floor or among the tree branches and trunks. The Lone Pine Field Guide's *Mammals of the Rocky Mountains* tells us that the fluidity of the marten's motions and its attractive appearance juxtapose its carnivorous and often swift hunting tactics. A keen predator, the American marten sniffs out voles, bird eggs and fledglings and acrobatically pursues red squirrels.

Unfortunately, this animal's playfulness, agility and insatiable curiosity are not easily observed, because they tend to inhabit wilder areas. I watched a television program on PBS about an older man in his mid-70s living off the land in Alaska, and he 'captured' a pine marten while he was out snowshoeing. Since it was lunchtime, he broke out a jar of strawberry jam, and the hyperactive marten calmed down and lapped up the jam out of the Mason jar. When he was done, the marten proceeded to thrash about uncontrollably like before.

Lions and Martens and Bears OH MY!

I never got to see a marten in my job, but I did survey for them using snowmobiles and track plates in northeast Oregon, one of the toughest jobs I ever had. I don't know how many times I had to dig out my snowmobile from deep snow. I'm glad I was younger then! More typically, martens are seen from the window of a vehicle flashing across a forest roadway or hiking on a backcountry trail.

Most widely known for its soft luxurious fur, the American marten is targeted on trap-lines in remote wilderness areas. As with many species of forest mammals, marked fluctuations seem to occur every few years. Evidence from trappers and their records suggest populations of these furbearers are definitely cyclical in nature.

The American marten is often used as an indicator of environmental conditions, because it depends upon food found in mature coniferous forests. Declining populations of this mustelid are indicators of a lack of food associated with loss of mature forests.

Also called a pine marten, the American marten is a slender-bodied, fox-faced weasel with a beautiful pale yellow to dark brown coat and a long, bushy tail. The feet are well-furred and equipped with strong non-retractile claws. The eyes are dark and almond-shaped. The Lone Pine Field Guide describes its breast spot, that when present, is usually orange but sometimes whitish or cream-colored. It tells us that it varies in size from a small dot to a large patch that occupies the entire region from the chin to the belly.

The male is about 15 percent larger than the female, uncommon in the mammal world. They have a well-developed scent gland, about 3-inches long and 1-inch wide on the center of the abdomen. As previously stated, American marten prefer mature coniferous forests that contain numerous dead trunks, branches and leaves to provide cover for its rodent prey. It does not occupy recently burned or cutover areas.

The preferred den site is a hollow tree or log that the female lines with dry grass and leaves. Breeding occurs in July or August, but with delayed implantation of the embryo, litters of one to six (usually three or four) young aren't born until March or April. The young are blind and almost naked at birth and totally dependent on their mother for survival until six or seven weeks of age. The mother must quickly teach her young to hunt, because when they are only about three months old she will re-enter estrus, and, with mating activity, the family group disbands. Or, as I like to say: *"Out with the old, in with the new!"*

Antlers

ELK LOCKING ANTLERS

Antlers are the large, branching, bony appendages on the heads of males of most deer species. Antler originally meant the lowest tine—the brow tine. It comes from the Old French *antoillier*, and possibly from the Latin word *anteocularis*, meaning 'before the eye.' Antlers are unique to cervids (deer) and found mostly on males; only caribou and reindeer have antlers on the females, and these are normally smaller than those of the males. So what's the deal with antlers?

Each antler grows from an attachment point on the skull, which is called a pedicile. While an antler is growing it is covered with highly vascular skin referred to as 'velvet,' which supplies oxygen and nutrients to the growing bone. Antlers grow faster than any other mammal bone. Once the antler has achieved its full size, the velvet is lost and the antler's bone dies. This dead bone structure is the mature antler.

Fastest-Growing Bone

In most cases, the bone at the base is destroyed, and the antler falls off at some point. As a result of their fast growth rate, antlers are considered a handicap since there is an incredible nutritional demand on deer or elk to re-grow antlers every year, and thus can be a good signal of food-gathering capability. My nephew Zeke just spent a weekend gathering sheds, also called shed antlers. These shed antlers usually accumulate in one area—areas often kept secret by those who hunt them. In the United States, sheds can fetch up to $100 each.

Shed antlers have been used by craftspeople since ancient times to make tools, weapons, ornaments, toys, and many other useful items. They are worn in traditional dances by indigenous peoples, such as the Deer Dance by Pueblo Indians. Back in the day, I remember going to watch the deer dances in the old meadow where the Wendy's burger joint now stands in Taos.

How does a horn differ from an antler? A horn is made of keratinized epithelium. Your fingernails are made of keratinized epithelium. It is hardened skin tissue (the fingernail) on top of bone (your fingers). A horn then is a pointed projection of hardened skin on the head of various animals, like pronghorn antelope, consisting of a covering of keratin and other proteins surrounding a core of live bone.

Antler velvet of deer and elk has been used in Asia as a dietary supplement or alternative medicine for more than 2,000 years. In prehistoric times, a large shed deer antler was often cut down to its shaft and its lowest tine (point) was used as a one-pointed pickax.

Bats

(Myotis Species)

LESSER HORSESHOE BAT

The most common bats of the temperate Northern Hemisphere are the cosmopolitan little brown bats *(Myotis lucifugus)*, big brown bats or serotines *(Eptesicus)*, and pipistrelles. There are over a dozen species of Myotis in North America; the common little brown bat is distributed over the entire continent from Alaska and Labrador to the southern United States. A colonial bat, it is found in many habitats, including houses.

I remember when I was working in my first job in Minnesota, I was living in an apartment above a pizza place. I was lying there in the dark trying to sleep, and I kept hearing this banging on the window next to the bed. It was a bat trying to escape outside! That was my first introduction to bats. Later in the summer we set up mist nets to capture and band the little flying mammals. Cool job. That's about the time I decided I was going to make wildlife biology my life's work. And to think I owe it all to a little brown bat.

Scary, Freaky, or Just Plain Amazing?

The free-tailed bats (family Molossidae) are a cosmopolitan group of communal bats characterized by a long tail extending well beyond the end of the tail membrane. The Brazilian free-tailed bat *(Tadarida brasiliensis)* is noted for its colonies in the Carlsbad Caverns of southern New Mexico, numbering an estimated 250,000 to 500,000 individuals. When these bats leave the caves at the same time, it takes about 20 minutes for the entire column to make its exit.

Hibernation is the one trait of bats that is probably most responsible for allowing an essentially tropical mammal to live year-round in temperate regions. Surveying bats in caves in the winter is a great way to estimate the total population, but it must be done very cautiously, because waking up a bat during its winter hibernation can spell doom for the critter.

In *Bats of the Rocky Mountains*, author Rick Adams explains that all bats are homeothermic, meaning they are capable of maintaining a constant and regulated body temperature, but also having the ability to survive, without injury or death, temperatures that vary substantially over a wide range. Back in Colorado, I once worked at a cave called the Oil Creek Tunnel, created by a miner in the 1800s. He attempted to dig a tunnel from Colorado Springs through Pikes Peak to get to Cripple Creek on the other side. He only got 150 feet or so into the mountain, but in doing so, created a heck of a place for bats to hibernate in the winter.

We discovered our greatest number and diversity of bats in Oil Creek Tunnel. But we also went to extreme lengths to keep people out and limit disturbance to the bats by installing what's known as a bat grate. This allowed bats to freely move in and out of the tunnel to hibernate but limited human curiosity and disturbance.

Like dolphins, most bats communicate and navigate with high-frequency sounds. This is called echolocation. Using sound alone, bats can 'see' everything but color in total darkness and can detect obstacles as fine as a human hair. The sophistication of their unique echolocation systems surpasses current scientific understanding. On a watt-per-watt, ounce-per-ounce basis, echolocation has been estimated to be literally billions of times more efficient than any similar system developed by humans. You know I have to say it: *don't ya just love nature!*

Bison

(Bison bison)

BISON

American bison, also known as the American buffalo, is comprised of two subspecies, the plains bison and the wood bison. Plains bison is the one we are most familiar with. Both species were hunted close to extinction during the 19th and 20th centuries but have since rebounded. The American plains bison is no longer listed as endangered, but the wood bison is on the Endangered Species List in Canada.

An American Original

In *American Bison: A Natural History* by Dale F. Lott, we learn bison are nomadic grazers and travel in herds. The bulls leave the herds of females at two or three years of age and join a male herd which is generally smaller than the female herds. Mature bulls rarely travel alone. Both sexes reunite for the mating season towards the end of summer. American bison tend to graze more and browse less; they favor head-butting as opposed to locking horns, and the American bison breed with domestic cattle more readily than wood bison. The number of bison remaining alive in North America declined to as low as 541 animals.

The U.S. National Bison Association has adopted a code of ethics that prohibits its members from deliberately crossbreeding bison with any other species. That's not to say that crossbreeding has not occurred in the past. During the time that they were on the brink of extinction, a handful of ranchers gathered remnants of the existing herds to save the species. These ranchers bred some of the bison with cattle and produced 'cattleo' and 'beefalo.' Accidental crossings were also known to occur over the years. Generally, male domestic bulls were crossed with buffalo cows, producing offspring of which only the females were fertile. The crossbred animals did not demonstrate any form of hybrid vigor, so the practice was abandoned.

Wallowing is a common behavior of bison. A bison wallow is a shallow depression in the soil, either wet or dry, that bison roll in and cover themselves with mud or dust to groom themselves, get relief from skin irritation due to biting insects, and to have good all-around play or fun. The bison's temperament is often unpredictable. They usually appear peaceful, unconcerned, and even lazy, yet they may attack anything, often without warning or apparent reason. Kind of like the State Farm TV commercial. At the time bison ran wild, they were rated second only to the Alaska brown bear as a potential killer, more dangerous than a grizzly bear! In *American Bison*, Lott relates the sentiments of early naturalists about bison: "They were a dangerous, savage animal that feared no other animal, and in prime condition could best any foe...except for maybe wolves and brown bears."

Knowing how many bison there were goes beyond casual curiosity. We can't understand the ecosystem of primitive North America, or the magnitude of the human rearrangement of that ecosystem, without a good estimate of the primitive North American bison population. Still, I have not found a definitive number in the literature—and believe me, I have looked. I have read that there were anywhere from 30 to 60 million bison in primitive North America. It's almost as though most authors fear taking a formal stance on the original number of bison in North America, or that we are just too embarrassed by the number.

Nevertheless, the book *Buffalo Nation: History and Legend of the North American Bison* (also authored by Dale Lott) chronicles with great detail the plight of the American bison in America. We should not be embarrassed, but we should learn from our mistakes.

Black Bear

(Ursus americanus)

A common inhabitant of forests in the Rocky Mountains, the black bear is often feared by city dwellers who come to the mountain parks to appreciate the scenery and wild areas. People who are more experienced with the forest and the behavior of animals, however, tend to regard the black bear with casual familiarity. In fact, the black bear is on the insignia of the New Mexico Department of Game and Fish, sort of a calling card for everything wild in our great state.

BLACK BEAR

New Mexico's State Mammal

Contrary to popular belief and their membership in the carnivore group of mammals, authors Fisher, Pattie and Hartson of *Mammals of the Rocky Mountains* inform us that black bears do not readily hunt larger animals. They are primarily opportunistic foragers and feed on what is easy and abundant, usually berries, horsetails, insects like ants in the summer, other vegetation, young deer fawns, or another carnivore's kill. They won't turn their nose up at fish.

Black bear sows (females) with cubs are the most likely to attack, even if unprovoked. In the past few decades, the infamous dandelion has become increasingly abundant in the mountains and along roadsides and as a result, black bears are now more frequently seen.

Within its territory, a black bear will have favorite feeding places and will follow well-traveled paths to these sites. Keep in mind that the paths you hike in the mountains may be used not only by other humans but also by bears wanting to get to lush meadows or rich berry patches.

Normally, black bears are peaceful, reclusive animals that will flee to avoid contact with humans. When Diane and I lived at the Manitou Experimental Forest in Colorado, a very large, 300+ pounds, cinnamon-colored black bear came wandering through the compound. We knew because our Siberian husky Sierra had a piercing bark when a wild animal was around, and she woke us up at 2:30 a.m. to see that bear!

Black bears mate in June or July, but their embryos do not implant until the sow enters her den in November. The number of eggs implanted seems to be correlated with the female's weight and condition; for example, fat mothers have more cubs (usually two or three). Young are born and nursed while the sow sleeps during hibernation. *Ain't nature grand!* The cubs' eyes open when they are five or six months old, and they leave the den with their mother when they weigh 4.5 to 6.5 pounds. The sow and her cubs generally spend the next winter together in the original den, dispersing the following spring. Black bears typically have young every other year.

One of the darkest threats to black bears throughout their range is the illegal aphrodisiac market. Also bears will be poached for their bear paws and gall bladders, which have very high black-market values.

Perhaps the most famous black bear of all is Smokey Bear. If we listen to Smokey, no other cub will suffer the way he did—orphaned, burned and made homeless by a fire! Let's all remember what Smokey says, "Only *you* can prevent forest fires."

Rocky Mountain Elk and Mule Deer

(Cervus elaphus nelsonii)

MULE DEER

Rocky Mountain Elk *(Cervus elaphus nelsoni)* and mule deer *(Odocoileus hemionus)* are among the few large animals that can convert green vegetation efficiently into animal protein. That specialty makes them important as meals for other animals, including humans; therefore they also specialize in the art of avoiding predators. These two dual specialties shape almost every attribute of these animals. Wild ungulates (warm-blooded, hoofed mammals) are central figures in the dance of life, and serve as living links among sun, soil, and sentient life, according to *Antlered Animals of the West* by Kevin Van Tighen. Their trails stitch together the living landscape of western North America.

Before the arrival of Europeans, Rocky Mountain elk were the most plentiful and widely distributed members of the deer family (Cervidae) in North America, said David Peterson in *Among the Elk*. Rocky Mountain elk, also known as 'wapiti' by Native Americans, is considered a 'conspecific' species to the European red deer. This means they are one and the same, but on different continents. They inhabited North America some 120,000 years ago by crossing the Bering land bridge, which once connected Siberia with Alaska.

Approximately 750,000 head of elk now inhabit the North American continent. This is but 7 percent of the estimated pre-Columbian population of 10 million. The Rocky Mountain elk now comprises four living subspecies. Two other races have gone extinct within this century. The elk might stretch 80 inches (6½ feet) from nose to rump, stand to around 55 inches (4.6 feet) at the shoulders, and weigh 700 to 900 pounds—overall about the size of a small horse.

While a few Rocky Mountain bull (male) elk in the half-ton class may still exist, they are as scarce as fur on a fish! Cow elk (females) average a couple hundred pounds lighter but may be the better tasting of the two. Now I started a war! The females also lead the herd, care for the young, and choose the routes to the wintering grounds. Now I *really* started a war!

Evidence indicates that Native Americans hunted elk as long as 11,000 years ago. The 'wapiti' was rarely the quarry of first choice for American Indians; however it was, in fact, an essential element in native diets and economies, said Peterson in *Among the Elk*.

Elk don't lead very complicated lives. You don't need to be a psychologist to figure out what motivates an elk. It can be summed up in three words: food, cover, and water. The average elk will eat about three pounds of food per day per 100 pounds of body weight, so you can quickly understand elk are going to need a lot of time to get the amount of food they need to survive. Elk are ungulates and have four stomachs, much like a domestic cow. The activity of eating by itself takes up a good portion of an elk's day, especially during fall, as an elk begins to prepare for limited food availability in winter.

Elk aren't just hunted by humans; they are prey to many other predators in the forest. If elk seem a bit skittish in general, it's for good reason. They must constantly have their guard up. Simply put, the best feed is going to grow in some of the least protected areas. Open areas. This is why elk will feed on the edges of meadows more often than in the middle, as they know that the safety of the thick timber is only a few steps away. Elk will get water from ponds, streams, springs, seeps, puddles left from rains and melted snow, and even from dew left behind on the leaves in the morning.

Ever been to Rocky Mountain National Park near Estes Park, Colorado in the fall? You can witness an amazing display of elk mating habits, from bugling, to sparring, even breeding. Whether you realize it or not, all living things are hard-wired to keep the gene pool going.

Mountain Lion

(Puma concolor)

MOUNTAIN LION

New Mexico is one of the last places in the United States where the species seems to be holding its own. Even mountains near large urban centers harbor a few lions; however, mountain lions are typically found in remote, wooded, rocky places, usually near an abundant supply of deer, their primary food source. In the Rocky Mountains, they inhabit mainly the montane woodlands, according to *Mammals of the Rocky Mountains.*

Mountain lions are also known by the common names cougar and puma. Both names are of South American Indian origin, the former from Amazonia and the latter from the Andes region. In *The Natural History of New Mexican Mammals,* J.S. Findley explains that the names of English origin include 'panther,' originally from Greek, and 'catamount,' which refers to other wild felids as well as the mountain lion. The term 'felids' is in reference to *Felidae*, the family name for mountain lions.

Lions and Martens and Bears, Oh My!

These large cats lead solitary lives, except for the association between mother and kittens, and between males and females at breeding time, typically in the spring. The males are promiscuous, staying with a given female only for the duration of her estrus. One to six young are born after 82 to 96 days. The young are weaned after six weeks, but they remain with their mother for up to two years, when they become sexually mature.

These large cats were once found throughout much of North

America, but conflicts with settlers and their stock animals resulted in widespread removal of this great feline. Again, *what a tangled web we weave!* Still, it is one of the most widespread, if not abundant, carnivores in both North and South America.

Although mountain lions are capable of great bursts of speed and giant leaps, they often opt for a less energy-intensive hunting strategy. Silent and nearly motionless, a mountain lion waits in ambush in a tree or on a ledge until prey approaches. I remember conducting Mexican spotted owl surveys at night in a very narrow, rocky canyon, and the hair on the back of my neck stood straight up. Next day I scouted the canyon in the daylight and ran across some cat hair on some bushes off the trail, and fresh mountain lion tracks at a nearby spring. Sent chills up my spine.

By leaping onto the shoulders of its prey and biting deep into the back of the neck while attempting to knock the prey off balance, the mountain lion can take down an animal as large as an adult elk. I don't think the air horn that I carried for safety purposes would have done me any good!

These big cats need the equivalent of about one deer a week to survive, and mountain lion densities in the Rocky Mountains tend to correlate with deer densities. Mountain lions are adaptable creatures that may hunt by day or by night.

The mountain lion, being one of the most charismatic animals of the Rocky Mountains, is a creature that every person hopes to see, from a safe distance of course! Which brings me to my next memory. While buying a log bed at a lumber mill next to the Manitou Experimental Forest, where I lived and worked in Colorado, I caught sight of an adult mountain lion tracking an elk that had been shot with an arrow during bow season. Few people—even field biologists—ever get more than a fleeting glimpse of these graceful felines.

Common Raccoon

(Procyon lotor)

RACCOON

There is nothing common about the Common raccoon, from his antics to the spelling of his name. Is it racoon or raccoon? I've seen it spelled both ways, and both ways seem correct to me. The *Encyclopedia of Animals* by Dr. Per Christiansen states that the raccoon is traditionally associated with wooded or swampy areas, and that its range has spread across southern Canada, the mainland United States, and as far south as Panama.

The raccoon can survive in open plains or in urban areas as long as there is water nearby. Probably the defining trait of the raccoon is the dark mask across his pointed face, but even that serves a purpose, besides making him look like Zorro. The *Encyclopedia of Animals* says that the mask probably helps to aid night vision: white fur would cause glare.

The Masked Bandit

The raccoon can use the long fingers of its dexterous forepaws to empty cans and operate latches; the bushy-ringed tail provides balance when the raccoon climbs and acts as a prop when the animal is sitting upright to feed. *Ain't nature grand!* The raccoon's dense, salt-and-pepper fur enables it to thrive in cold climates like northern New Mexico. Soft but durable, the pelt is also prized by trappers and fur traders who fashion it into warm hats and coats.

A raccoon is likely to investigate tasty bits of food and any shiny object that it finds. For all of its roguish behavior, however, the raccoon has never been associated with ferociousness or savagery—it is mainly a playful and gentle animal, unless it is cornered, threatened or rabid. *Mammals of the Rocky Mountains* states that raccoons are among the most frequently encountered wild carnivores in the southern Rocky Mountains. Actually, they are omnivores because they eat a little of everything, a critter after my own heart!

Albert Ortega, a good friend of mine and a fly-fisherman, was telling me a raccoon was 'fishing' underneath some boulders on the Red River, and that he typically sees them through November and into December. The way that raccoons typically 'feel' their way through the world has long been recognized, according to *Mammals of the Rocky Mountains*. In fact, our word raccoon is derived from the Algonquin Indian name for this animal "*aroughcounce*" which means "he scratches with his hands."

One of the best-known characteristics of the raccoon is its habit of dunking its food in water before eating it. It had long been thought that the raccoon was washing its food; in fact, the scientific name *lotor* is Latin for 'washer'. Today, biologists believe that a raccoon's sense of touch is enhanced by water, and that it is actually feeling for inedible bits to discard. Again: *Ain't nature grand!*

Common Porcupine

(Erethizon dorsatum)

PORCUPINE

With impressive defensive adaptations and exceptional climbing skills, the North American porcupine is highly successful in its wooded habitat, according to Dr. Per Christiansen in *The Encyclopedia of Animals*. Dr. Christiansen says the porcupine has about 30,000 quills which are thick, sharp, modified hairs. The tip of each quill is covered with microscopic, backward-pointing barbs that hold the quill fast and cause it to work its way deeper into the flesh of whatever poor, unsuspecting critter happened to alarm the porcupine.

The Spiny Pig of North America

Fisher, Pattie and Hartson in *Mammals of the Rocky Mountains* state that, contrary to popular belief, the porcupine cannot throw its quills, but if it is attacked or threatened, it will lower its head in a defensive posture and lash out with its tail. The loosely rooted quills will detach easily so that they may be driven deeply into the attacker's flesh. My Siberian husky, Sierra, could tell you all about her painful experience with a porcupine near Steamboat Springs, Colorado if she were alive today.

The range of the porcupine covers most of North America, from Alaska and Canada to northern Mexico, although Dr. Christiansen says it is absent from parts of the central and southern United States. Porcupines inhabit montane forests, foothills and even prairie environments in the mountains. They are completely herbivorous, the arboreal (tree-loving) counterpart of the American Beaver. It eats leaves, buds, twigs and especially young bark of both broadleaf and coniferous trees and shrubs.

Craig Childs states in *The Animal Dialogues* that there are two things a porcupine body does well: climbs trees and digests them. Nearly a third of its body weight is made up of digestive organs capable of breaking down the complex ingredients of leaves and bark. A great deal of time is spent resting and processing the leaves that it crawled to the branch's end to eat, which explains their apparent lack of motivation.

Porcupines are not lazy; they are just 'survival-motivated.' I suppose if you wore a fur coat made of thousands of needles, you'd move slowly and deliberately also. Don't be misled by their casual manner of hanging from trees far overhead; they are no daredevils. Porcupines do fall. Some falls result in death, others in quill heaps at the base of trees.

A little known fact about porcupine quills is that they do contain an antibiotic. Why antibiotic quills? If you are going to stab your enemy, it makes little sense to clean the knife first. The purpose lies elsewhere than in the wellbeing of a quill-infested coyote muzzle. If you fall 30 feet out of a tree wearing a coat of 30,000 needles, and you survive that, you don't want to die of infected stab wounds from your own fur coat. The word porcupine comes from the Old French word *porcespin*, which means spiny pig. The porcupine's genus/species name, Erethizon dorsatum, can be loosely translated as "the animal with the irritating back." I'd say that's pretty accurate.

In *Medicine Cards* by Jamie Sams and David Carson, we learn the medicine wheel is central to understanding the concept of medicine in the Native American way. The South direction of the medicine wheel is the place of childlike innocence and humility. It is the position of the porcupine on the medicine wheel of life. The two principal qualities of the porcupine are the power of faith and the power of trust. When fear is not present, it is possible to feed a porcupine by hand and never get stuck by its quills, although I personally have never tried that!

Coyote

(Canis latrans)

I grew up on the Bugs Bunny and Roadrunner cartoons on Saturday mornings. They were a hoot but had an element of truth in each episode, believe it or not. The chorus of yaps, whines, barks and howls was what I went to sleep to, and woke up to on occasion. Although coyote calls are most intense during late winter and spring, corresponding to courtship, these maniacal sounds can be heard during suitable weather at any time of the day or year.

COYOTE PUP

The Real Wile E. Coyote!

Often initiated by a single animal, many family groups soon join in, and the calls pour in from every direction, making it obvious to all that these animals like getting together and making noise. Fisher, Pattie and Hartson state in their book *Mammals of the Rocky Mountains* that when Lewis and Clark traveled through the Rocky Mountain wilderness two centuries ago, they made frequent references in their journal entries to foxes and wolves, but they seldom mentioned coyotes.

Coyotes have increased their numbers across North America in the past century in response to the expansion of agriculture and forestry and the reduction of wolf populations. Despite widespread human efforts to exterminate them, they have thrived—kind of like Wile E. Coyote!

Because of its relatively small size, the coyote typically preys on small animals such as mice, voles, ground squirrels, small birds and rabbits, but it has also been known to prey on bighorn sheep and mule deer, particularly their young. Although they normally hunt alone, they occasionally form packs, especially when they hunt hoofed mammals during the winter. The coyotes may split up, with some waiting in ambush while the others chase the prey toward them, or they may run in relays to tire their quarry.

The coyote—which is the best runner among North American canids (dogs)—typically cruises along at 25 to 30 miles per hour. Coyotes owe their modern-day success to their varied diet, early age at first breeding, high reproductive output and flexible living requirements. They consume carrion (dead stuff) throughout the year, but they also feed on such diverse offerings as eggs, cactus fruits, melons, vegetation and berries. Their variable diet and nonspecific habitat choices allow them to adapt to just about any region of North America.

Coyotes can and do interbreed with domestic dogs. The 'coydog' offspring often become nuisance animals, killing domestic livestock and poultry. Coyotes usually have a litter of five to seven pups born between late March and late May and occupy a den, which is usually a burrow in a slope, frequently an American badger or woodchuck hole that has been expanded to 1 foot in diameter and about 10 feet deep.

Yellow-bellied Marmot

(Marmota flaviventris)

YELLOW-BELLIED MARMOT

Also called a rock chuck and by its more colorful name the whistle-pig, marmots are found at Wheeler Peak and elsewhere above timberline near Taos. True to its name, the yellow-bellied marmot has a distinct yellowish or burnt-orange belly. When this marmot is curious about or watchful of something, it often sits on its hind legs in an upright position that displays its delightfully bright tummy.

Yellow-bellied marmots sleep late, eat heartily and then snooze dreamily on warm rocks in the sun after they emerge from their burrows, we learn in *Mammals of the Rocky Mountains.* Counting hibernation and nighttime sleep, yellow-bellied marmots spend about 80 percent of their lives beneath the ground in their burrows.

The Whistle-pigs

They like their dens to be kept clean, and when they emerge from hibernation they throw out their used grass bedding and replace it with fresh grass. Throughout the summer they continue to 'change the sheets' and keep their bedding clean and their burrows free of debris. Vernon Bailey's *Mammals of the Southwestern United States* says the Taos Indians call them "*pean-che-hah'na.*"

The yellow-bellied marmot is a true hibernator. During hibernation, its heart slows to between four to seven beats per minute, and it breathes in and out about once a minute. Its body temperature drops to 40 degrees or lower. It lies curled tightly in a ball with its paws over its eyes. According to *New Mexico Game and Fish Wildlife Notes*, the marmot very effectively survives the half-year long winters of the high mountains when no food is available. *Ain't nature grand!*

Depending on local conditions, marmots may enter hibernation from as early as late August to early October and emerge in March or April, or later. The young are born in late April and early May to give them maximum eating time before their first hibernation; there are from three to eight in a litter.

So why 'whistle-pig,' you might ask? Colonies of yellow-bellied marmots have a strict social order, and whenever members of a colony are eating or wrestling with their family members, at least one marmot plays watchdog. This sentinel is responsible for warning the others if danger approaches. The alarm call is a loud chirp, which may vary in duration and intensity depending on the nature of the threat; short, steady notes probably translate as "Everyone, pay attention—something is wrong." Loud, shrill notes convey the message: "Into your burrows, *now*!"

Different urgent warnings are reserved for immediate dangers, such as a circling golden eagle or an approaching fox. Within the Rockies, marmot population sizes seem to be regulated by the availability of suitable hibernation sites. A burrow is typically 8 to 14 inches in diameter, slants down for 20 to 40 inches, and then extends another 10 to 15 feet to end beneath or among large rocks in a bulky nest lined with grass.

I had a very memorable experience near the top of Pikes Peak in Colorado when I was the District Biologist there. I was having a media event to show off three new bighorn sheep signs we had just installed. It had been cold and windy all week leading up to the media day, and there were no bighorns to be seen. But on the day of the event, the sun was shining on a beautiful summer day, a small herd of bighorns camped out right by the signs, and a yellow-bellied marmot stood on a nearby rock as if to welcome us. It couldn't have been more perfect!

Pika

(Ochotona princeps)

PIKA

Huddled motionless on a rock, the pika is difficult to spot; consequently, hikers usually hear them chirp before seeing them. "The ventriloquist qualities of its call mask the source of the sound," says Jan L. Wassink in *Mammals of the Central Rockies*. Uttered at the first sign of danger, the call is picked up by nearby pikas and echoed throughout the colony. If danger comes too close, the little animal disappears beneath an overhanging rock or between the rocks in the boulder field.

The comical little pika, alias "cony" or "rock rabbit," is a widespread and typical resident of the Rocky Mountains, occurring southward to Taos County and Northern New Mexico. I've seen pika near the summit of Wheeler Peak and Culebra Peak. Outwardly the pika shows little resemblance to the rabbit, but the relationship is clear when skulls and teeth are compared.

The Little Rabbit That Could

Pikas are not to be seen just anywhere in the Rockies. "They are extremely selective about habitat," according to *Wildlife in the Rockies*, by George Brybycin. Rockslides, otherwise known as talus slopes, are the only home of pikas, although they will travel short distances into nearby meadows or brush to procure food consisting entirely of vegetation. The pika is not likely to be confused with any other mammal. Aside from its specialized habitat, pika characteristics include its small size (about 6 ounces in weight and 6 to 8 inches in length), no visible tail, and short rounded ears.

The tiny pikas are known as nature's haymakers. The pika has an interesting strategy for survival in its harsh alpine environment. It neither hibernates like many high mountain rodents, nor scurries about searching for food all year like its distant cousins the hares.

It prefers instead to gather a large cache of food during the short summer months, which it stores in its rocky hideaway for winter sustenance. Pikas are active only during the day, remaining so all year-round, although winter activity is confined to the den and their immediate vicinity. The winter food supply is picked green in the summer and placed in little piles here and there on the rocks near the winter den so that it will cure in the sun. These odd-looking little haystacks are sure evidence that the bustling little pikas are close at hand.

The haystacks are popularly thought to consist of grass, but in fact many plants are used such as ferns, sedges, hellebore, lily-of-the-valley, aspen, willow, mountain ash, serviceberry, columbine, clover and bluebells. During feeding pikas tend to make short rapid forays from the talus slopes, rarely straying more than 5 meters (16+ feet).

Pronghorn

(Antilocapra Americana)

PRONGHORN

Although sometimes called antelope, pronghorn are not closely related to the animals of the African Plains. In fact, they are so different from other hoofed animals that they are the only members of the family Antilocapridae, according to the U.S. Fish and Wildlife Service. Their head ornaments set them apart from deer and elk whose branched, solid antlers are shed each year, and from goats and cattle whose hollow horns are made from hair and are not shed. Pronghorn have branched, hollow, hair-like horns that are shed annually. They are the only animal with this combination.

True Americans

True Americans, pronghorn are found only on the plains and grasslands of North America. I remember when I lived near Divide, Colorado, there was a small band of pronghorn that lived in a wide, grassy meadow between Divide and Woodland Park. These animals had been transplanted from the plains east of Colorado Springs and were thriving in a very small patch of suitable habitat. Unfortunately, they fell to habitat development, as the next large subdivision now occupies the site.

Like bison, seemingly endless numbers once covered the plains and grasslands of the West, stretching from Saskatchewan, Canada, through the western United States, down to Mexico City in Mexico. And like bison, they nearly became extinct. Before the end of the prairie and of the vast number of bison, there may have been as many as 50 million pronghorn in North America in the early 1800s, dwindling to less than 15,000 by 1915. A moratorium on hunting lasting until the 1940s, a federal tax on firearms and sporting goods, and funding for conservation efforts, are all credited with stopping the extinction of the pronghorn. I wish I could've been a fly on the wall in the early 1800s.

Today, there are almost one million Pronghorn. Five subspecies are now recognized. Most pronghorn are found on grasslands receiving 10 to 15 inches of rainfall per year, at between 4,000 and 6,000 feet elevation. Pronghorn need open, flat valleys to make use of their most famous attributes—speed and eyesight, according to the U.S. Fish and Wildlife Service.

Vegetation must not exceed 30 inches so approaching predators are visible to them, and with eyes almost as large as an elephant's on a body the size of a goat, pronghorn are clearly designed for watchfulness.

They nap throughout the day, waking to take a look now and then, and once alerted, they can outrun any potential predator fairly easily. The herd travels as one, not leaving a single animal open to attack. They keep the pace up for several miles, their speed and endurance resulting from the pressure of their traditional enemy the wolf.

Slower solitary hunters, coyotes pose a threat only in the first few weeks when a fawn's best defense is invisibility, but as many as 50 percent of a year's fawns may be lost to coyotes and other predators. Does leave deer-colored newborn fawns hidden in the grass, returning to nurse them for 30 seconds every five hours. What appears to be abandonment actually increases their chances of not being detected.

Probably the coolest trait I learned about pronghorn is that when they are running and come to a barbed-wire fence they actually go *under* the fence, unlike a mule deer who bounds *over* the fence! Again: *Ain't nature grand!*

Red Fox

(Vulpes vulpes)

RED FOX CUBS

The red fox is the largest of the true foxes and the most geographically widespread member of the order Carnivora, being distributed across the entire northern hemisphere from the Arctic Circle to North Africa, Central America and Asia. Not to be mistaken for Redd Fox, the famous actor of the TV series *"Sanford and Son"* in the 1970s, the red fox has a long history of association with humans, having been extensively hunted and trapped as a furbearer for centuries, as well as being prominently represented in human folklore and mythology.

The Trickster

Apart from its large size, the red fox is distinguished from 45 other fox species by its ability to adapt quickly to new environments and, unlike most of its cousins, is not listed as an endangered species anywhere. Despite its name, the species often produces individuals with abnormal colorings, including albinos and melanists. Typically though, the red fox has orangish-red fur on its back, sides and head, with white fur under its neck and on its chest. It has a long bushy tail tipped in white, pointed black ears, and black legs and feet.

The red fox makes its home in wooded areas, prairies, farmlands, and nowadays, urban open spaces. The red fox eats a wide variety of foods. It is an omnivore, and its diet includes fruits, berries, grasses, birds, and small mammals like squirrels, rabbits and mice. A large part of the red fox's diet is made up of invertebrates like crickets, caterpillars, grasshoppers, beetles and crayfish. The red fox will continue to hunt even when it is full. It stores extra food under leaves, dirt or snow.

The red fox mates from January through March, with the female making one or more dens right after mating. A little less than two months after mating, the female gives birth to a litter of between one and ten kits. The male brings the female food while she is caring for the kits, and the kits start playing outside the den when they are about a month old. When they are a few weeks old, the mother will bring them live prey to 'play with' and eat. Playing with live prey helps the young kits develop the skills they will need for hunting. The kits leave their mother when they are about seven months old.

The red fox is mostly nocturnal, although it will sometimes venture out in the day. The red fox, unlike other mammals, hears low-frequency sounds very well. It can hear a mouse digging underground and will frequently dig in the dirt or snow to catch prey. The fox stalks its prey, much like a cat, and gets as close as it can before pouncing on its unsuspecting victim.

Except for breeding females, the fox does not usually use a den. Often it will sleep in the open, wrapping its bushy tail around its nose to stay warm. When it does use a den, it will usually find an abandoned rabbit or marmot den instead of making its own den.

Red foxes feature prominently in the folklore and mythology of human cultures with which they are sympatric. In later European folklore, the figure of 'Reynard the Fox' symbolizes trickery and deceit. Chinese folk tales tell of fox-spirits called *huli jing* that may have up to nine tails. In Japanese mythology, the *kitsune* are foxlike spirits possessing magical abilities that increase with their age and wisdom. Foremost among these is the ability to assume human form. While some folktales speak of *kitsune* employing this ability to trick others, other stories portray them as faithful guardians, friends, lovers and wives. The cunning fox is commonly found in Native American mythology, where it is portrayed as an almost constant companion to the coyote. Fox, however, is a deceitful companion who often steals coyote's food.

Bighorn Sheep

(*Ovis canadensis*)

BIGHORN SHEEP

"Regal" is the word that has always spoken bighorn sheep to me! It means kingly, royal, or magnificent, and is perhaps the reason this has always been my favorite North American mammal since I was a kid watching "*Marty Stouffer's Wild America*" on PBS.

Bighorn males, called rams, are famous for their large, curled horns. These impressive growths are a symbol of status and a weapon used in epic battles across the Rocky Mountains according to National Geographic's *Keep It Wild* magazine. Fighting for dominance or mating rights, the rams face each other, rear up on their hind legs, and hurl themselves at each other in charges of some 20 mph. The resounding clash of horns can be heard echoing through the mountains as the confrontation is repeated—sometimes for many hours—until one ram submits and walks away. The animal's thick, bony skull usually prevents serious injury.

A Regal Treat

According to Burt & Grossenheider in *A Field Guide to Mammals*, the bighorn ram's horns can weigh 30 pounds, the world record being 33 pounds—more than all the other bones in his body combined! Females, called ewes, also have horns, but they are much smaller in size. They typically have one lamb (rarely two), and they are able to stand, run, and climb shortly after they are born. In *Mammals of North America* by Bowers & Kaufman, we learn that bighorn sheep are surefooted animals found in high alpine meadows to low deserts—wherever grassy areas for feeding are close to the steep rocky terrain they need to escape predators.

I recall the bighorn sheep herd in Queen's Canyon on the Pikes Peak Ranger District in Colorado Springs. This herd was extirpated in the early 1900s but through increased protection and a vigorous transplant program, the herd is now stable at 350 animals. This herd is different from the herd on top of Pikes Peak, and different from the herd in the Tarryall Mountains 30 miles to the west of Pikes Peak. Extirpated means they were eradicated or exterminated, back in the days of market hunting and little thought toward preservation or conservation.

In *The Living World of Audubon Mammals,* Robert Elman notes that bighorn sheep do not pick their way through rough terrain like mountain goats but instead bound from point to point on sharp-rimmed, spongy, slightly concave hooves. Their vision is said to equal that of a man aided by eight power binoculars. Lambs are dropped (born) in the spring and remain with the bands of ewes (or groups of ewes) for a couple of years before the young males form "bachelor bands" of their own.

The Foundation for North American Wild Sheep (FNAWS) was founded in 1977 and is now the fastest-growing wildlife conservation organization of its kind, with a mission to be "the best managed, most respected, and most influential conservation organization in the world." Their purpose is "to put and keep sheep on the mountain."

Fish

Rio Grande Cutthroat Trout

(Onchorhyncus clarkii virginialus)

The State fish of New Mexico, the Rio Grande cutthroat trout (cutts) has been the focus of most conservation work in New Mexico by the New Mexico Council of Trout Unlimited (TU), and in particular the Enchanted Circle Chapter of TU (ECTU) in Taos.

RIO GRANDE CUTTHROAT TROUT

State Fish of New Mexico

There is a perception that Rio Grande cutts are small fish. This perception comes from the fact that they have been relegated to tiny headwater streams either by habitat degradation or competition from non-native brown trout and/or rainbow trout. This actually is incorrect. Rio Grande cutts can grow into large trophy fish given the right conditions.

TU currently sits on the Rio Grande Cutthroat Trout Working Group, which consists of representatives from the NM Department of Game and Fish (NMDGF), US Forest Service (USFS), US Fish and Wildlife Service (USFWS), the Interstate Stream Commission (ISC), and other Non-Governmental Agencies. The objective of this group is to make sure that restoration efforts continue to move forward, that they include input from all agencies, and that these efforts have the best chance of being successful.

In May 2008, the USFWS determined that the Rio Grande cutthroat trout should be listed under the Endangered Species Act. The current status of the fish is as a "Candidate" species, meaning the Service will officially list the fish when it can complete the necessary paperwork.

ECTU has grown from their humble beginning of 33 members in 2007 to well over 100 members today. The local chapter is working with NMDGF to restore habitat to the lower Red River, continue working on a project to protect native Rio Grande cutthroat trout in the Hondo watershed, and continue support for outreach programs like Casting for Recovery and Project Healing Waters.

Northern Pike

(Esox lucius)

NORTHERN PIKE

The Northern pike, known simply as a pike in Britain, Ireland, and most parts of the U.S., jackfish in Canada, or simply northern in the Upper Midwest, is a species of carnivorous fish of the genus Esox (the pikes). They are typical of brackish and fresh waters in the Northern Hemisphere. In addition, pike are confined to the low salinity water at the surface of the Baltic Sea, and are seldom ever seen in brackish water elsewhere.

Pike are found in 31 U.S. states and in six Canadian provinces, and have been introduced to some Western lakes and reservoirs for angling purposes, although some fisheries managers believe this practice often threatens other species of fish such as bass, trout, and salmon, causing government agencies to attempt to exterminate the pike by poisoning and other means.

Northern pike are most often olive green in color. The flanks of the fish are marked with short, light bar-like spots, and the lower half of the gill cover lacks scales. They have large sensory pores on their head and underside of the lower jaw. Pike grow to a relatively large size; lengths of 59 inches and weights of 55 pounds are not unheard of. The majority of pike over 18 pounds are females.

Predator Extraordinaire

Pike are typical ambush predators. They lie in wait for prey to come along, holding perfectly still for long periods, then exhibit remarkable acceleration as they strike. Pike are spring spawners. The males are first to the spawning grounds, preceding the females by a week or two. Under natural conditions, the survival from free-swimming larvae to about 2.5 inches is around 5 percent. Pike normally live 5 to 15 years, but they can get as old as 30 years.

The young free-swimming pike feed on small invertebrates. When the body length reaches about 2.3 inches they start feeding on small fish. The pike has a distinctive habit of catching its prey sideways in its mouth, immobilizing it with its sharp backward-pointing teeth, and then turning the prey headfirst to swallow it. The pike will also feed on water voles, ducklings, frogs, insects and leeches. They are not very particular, and eat spiny fish like perch.

I've spent quite a bit of time talking about the feeding habits of the pike. You would understand if you ever caught a northern pike while fishing. The teeth of a pike are quite memorable. As a kid, my dad and my brothers and I went fishing at Miami Lake near Cimarron, New Mexico. Steel leaders, which I must say, I had never used before, were a must. Although, the pike caught in the picture was caught on a fly-fishing rig near the John Dunn Bridge on the Rio Grande near Taos. So I guess you just never know!

The Northern pike is a largely a solitary predator. Sometimes scuba-divers observe groups of similar-sized pike that might show some co-operation, and it is known to anglers that pike tend to start hunting at the same time, so there are some wolf pack theories about that. Pike are often found near the exit of a culvert, which can be attributed to the presence of schools of prey fish and the opportunity for ambush.

Although generally known as a sporting quarry, some anglers release pike they've caught because the flesh is considered bony, especially due to the substantial Y-bones they possess. Larger fish are more easily fileted. Pike have a long and distinguished history as cuisine and are popular fare in Europe. Historical references to cooking pike go as far back as the Romans. The flesh is white and mild-tasting. Fishing for pike is said to be very exciting, with their aggressive hits and aerial acrobatics. Pike are among the largest North American freshwater game fish.

Rainbow Trout

Wild rainbows can often be identified when hooked. They instantly jump or have a powerful surge that pen-raised fish don't have. They also tend to be brighter in color, and most of the smaller wild ones are decorated with "par markings," which appear as faint fingerprints on the side. Another telltale sign of a wild rainbow is its pink fins with white tips.

Rainbow trout prosper where there are profuse food sources. They tend to occupy and feed in the main channels and riffles of rivers where such food is funneled. They feed better in warmer waters than other trout.

— EXCERPT FROM *INSTINCTIVE FLY FISHING* BY TAYLOR STREIT

RIAINBOW TROUT

The rainbow trout is native only to the rivers and lakes of North America but its value as a hard-fighting game fish and tasty meal has led to its introduction throughout the world.

Rainbow trout are gorgeous fish, with color patterns that vary widely depending on habitat, age, and spawning condition. They are torpedo-shaped and generally blue-green or silver-green in color with a pink streak along their sides, white underbelly, and small black spots on their back and fins.

They are members of the salmon family and, like their salmon cousins, can grow quite large. They average about 20 to 30 inches in length as an adult.

Freshwater resident rainbow trout usually inhabit and spawn in small to moderately large, well-oxygenated, shallow rivers with gravel bottoms. They are native to the alluvial or freestone streams that are typical of tributaries of the Pacific basin. Lake resident rainbow trout are usually found in moderately deep, cool lakes with adequate shallows and vegetation to support production of sufficient food sources.

Lake populations generally require access to gravelly-bottomed streams to be self-sustaining, and in rivers spawning sites are usually a bed of fine gravel in a riffle above a pool. A female trout clears a redd (nest) in the gravel by turning on her side and beating her tail up and down. Female rainbow trout usually produce 2,000 to 3,000 four-to-five millimeter eggs per kilogram of weight. During spawning, the eggs fall into spaces between the gravel, and immediately the female begins digging at the upstream edge of the nest, covering the eggs with the displaced gravel. As eggs are released by the female, a male rainbow moves alongside and deposits milt (sperm) over the eggs to fertilize them.

The eggs usually hatch in about four to seven weeks although the time of hatching varies greatly with region and habitat. Newly hatched trout are called sac-fry or alevin. In approximately two weeks, the yolk sac is completely consumed and fry commence feeding mainly on zooplankton. The growth rate of rainbow trout is variable with area, habitat, life history, and quality and quantity of food.

As fry grow, they begin to develop "parr" marks or dark vertical bars on their sides. These small juvenile trout are sometimes called fingerlings because they are approximately the size of a human finger. In streams where rainbow trout are stocked for sport fishing but no natural reproduction occurs, some of the stocked trout may survive and grow or "carryover" for several seasons before they are caught or perish.

The ocean-going form of rainbow trout, called anadromous, including those returning for spawning, are known as steelhead in Canada and the U.S. Like salmon, steelhead return to their original hatching grounds to spawn. Similar to Atlantic salmon, but unlike their Pacific *Oncorhynchus* salmonid kin, steelhead are iteroparous (able to spawn several times, each time separated by months) and make several spawning trips between fresh and salt water, although fewer than

10 percent of native spawning adults survive from one spawning to another.

As young steelhead transition from freshwater to saltwater, a process called smoltification occurs where the trout undergoes physiological changes to allow it to survive in seawater. There are a number of genetic differences between freshwater rainbow trout and steelhead populations that may account for the smoltification in steelhead.

Rainbow trout are predators with a varied diet and will eat nearly anything they can capture. They are not as piscivorous (fish-eating) or aggressive as brown trout. Rainbow trout, including juvenile steelhead in fresh water, routinely feed on larval, pupal, and adult forms of aquatic insects (typically caddisflies, stoneflies, mayflies, and aquatic diptera).

They also eat fish eggs and adult forms of terrestrial insects (typically ants, beetles, grasshoppers and crickets) that fall into the water. Other prey include small fish up to one-third of their length, crayfish, shrimp, and other crustaceans. As rainbow trout grow, though, the proportion of fish consumed increases in most populations. Some lake-dwelling forms may become plankton feeders. In rivers and streams populated with other salmonid species, rainbow trout eat varied fish eggs, including those of salmon, brown and cutthroat trout, and the eggs of other rainbow trout. Rainbows also consume decomposing flesh from carcasses of other fish. Adult steelhead in the ocean feed primarily on other fish and squids.

Brown Trout

(*Salmo trutta*)

BROWN TROUT

The brown trout was first introduced in the United States in 1883 from Germany and have since expanded to nearly every state in the union. That explains why I always called them "German browns" as a kid.

The Fish with an Attitude

The brown trout is a beautiful fish, similar in general shape to their cousin the salmon; the back is dark, sides are pale, and both sides are flecked with reddish spots that have pale borders. The belly is a creamy yellowish white. Juveniles and immature adults can be distinguished as they have bluish-grey spots, and adult males have a strongly curved lower jaw called a kype.

Trout, in general, are far and away the most popular game fish pursued by fly fishermen in New Mexico according to Craig Martin, editor of *Fly Fishing in Northern New Mexico*. Some trout can survive at surprisingly warm water temperatures. Browns and rainbows, for instance, live in streams where water temperatures sometimes rise into the mid-60s. But at high temperatures, they usually feed very little, their growth rate slows, and their resistance to disease diminishes. The maximum-recorded life span of a wild brown trout is five years.

All the same, Dick Sternberg states in *Fly Fishing for Trout in Streams* that all streams that support permanent trout populations have one thing in common: a reliable source of cold water.

As previously mentioned, brown trout are one of the most tolerant trout when it comes to water temperatures. They can thrive on water temperatures as warm as of 60 to 65 degrees Fahrenheit, whereas Arctic Char in Alaska can only thrive in water temperatures of 45 to

50 degrees Fahrenheit.

The brown trout, however, is the most cover-oriented of all trout, according to Sternberg. Brown trout often hold tight to cover during the day, then come out to feed at night.

In Taylor Streit's book *Instinctive Fly Fishing*, the author states, "This is a fish with a proclivity toward unrestrained aggression." In other words, they fight with an attitude! Mr. Streit advises to "look for big browns where the current has undercut earthen banks, rocks, and tree roots. Those slimy devils like working undercover."

Such spots are especially favored in late summer when rivers are low and hiding places scarce. The lusher the bank's grass, the happier the fish will be because there will be more shade and terrestrial insects. These spots are good choices during bright sunlight when the trout feel more comfortable tucked away under something.

I remember when I was in high school, the dad of my high school sweetheart used to take us fishing at "the riffles" on the Rio Grande near Taos. I never caught a thing fly fishing, but he always came back with a creel-full of fat brown trout. He has since passed on, but he will always hold cool memories in my book, him and his late 1950s Willy's Jeep truck with the wooden plank bed. Ah…memories!

Invertebrates

Western Tiger Swallowtail Butterfly

(*Papilio rutulus*)

WESTERN TIGER SWALLOWTAIL BUTTERFLY

Butterflies are nature's canvases with the gift of flight, a traveling art show of the air.

Swallowtail butterflies are large, colorful butterflies that form the family Papilionidae. There are over 550 species. Although the majority of these are tropical, members of Papilionidae are found in all continents except Antarctica. How do I find butterflies? Location. Location. Location. The most productive habitats for butterflies, those that have the greatest diversity of species and the largest number of individuals, are open areas with natural vegetation. Butterflies like sunshine.

Nature's Canvas with the Gift of Flight

The caterpillar is green, enlarged in front, and marked near the head with four yellow dots and two yellowish eye spots with bluish centers. The neck is banded with black and yellow, and the body has several rows of tiny blue dots. The caterpillar turns brownish in the last stage prior to pupation. It can reach a maximum length of two inches.

Butterfly diversity will usually be correlated with the complexity of the landscape. A stream or ditch running through the property is like gold. Almost all butterflies are active exclusively during the day, while the great majority of moths are active only at night. Western tiger swallowtail butterfly is widely distributed in woodlands and meadows, including suburban areas, especially near watercourses. They are found June through July.

Swallowtails differ from all other butterflies in that they have a unique organ behind their heads called an osmeterium. Normally hidden, this forked structure can be seen clearly when the caterpillar is threatened, or it can be forced out with a gentle squeeze, and emits smelly secretions containing terpenes.

Each butterfly goes through four distinct stages in its life: 1) egg, 2) caterpillar, 3) pupa (chrysalis), and 4) adult. This process of great physical change, or metamorphosis, has captured the imagination of people throughout the world, and many native peoples have myths and gods based upon those butterfly transformations. The ancient Mexicans considered the butterfly important enough to dedicate an entire palace to it at Teotihuacan, just outside Mexico City. They named this special site the "Palace of the Mariposa," *mariposa* being Spanish for butterfly.

Tarantula

(*Tarantula Genus*)

TARANTULA

Fearsome looking, the tarantulas—diverse and largest of the spiders—hold a special place in the folklore of cultures across the world. Its body and legs are hairy, body size is up to 3-inches long and 3-inches tall, leg span of up to 5 inches, eight marginally functional eyes in two groups on the forehead, mouth and two backward-pointing fangs below the eyes, eight legs on either side of a fused head and thorax...sounds like something from a horror show!

Fearsome Looking But Harmless

According to Jay Sharp at DesertUSA.com, there are about 850 species of tarantulas worldwide, with over 50 species of tarantulas, genus *Aphonopelma*, native to the southwestern and central portions of the United States. This includes several undescribed species (unknown to science). They can be found in 12 states west of the Mississippi River and south of the Missouri River.

Tarantulas "wander" at different times of year. Depending on the species, many have a more or less set mating season. The time frame in and around Taos is August through October each year. Typically, in the southwestern US, tarantulas live in solitude in desert basins, mountain foothills and forested slopes, and they occupy various kinds of 'nests,' with many species taking up residence in burrows or crevices, which may be sequestered in the ground, along cliff faces, among rocks, under tree bark, or in-between tree roots *(DesertUSA.com)*.

Some surround the entrance to their burrow with a silken 'welcome mat,' which vibrates like guitar strings and sends signals to the spider cloistered there, if potential prey should touch the strands. "A tarantula will attack literally anything that it can subdue: beetles, grasshoppers, locusts, other spiders, small lizards and mice," says biologist Fred Punzo (in *Tarantulas: A Complete Introduction*, by Al Davis). Tarantulas kill prey by injecting venom through their fangs into their prey.

During mating season, which varies from spring through fall, depending on the species and conditions, the males leave their burrows, sometimes *en masse*, to seek willing females. A male, encountering the silk surrounding the entrance to a female's burrow, calls and dances amorously. He may be rejected or embraced. In either event, he may get eaten, becoming "a readily available source of protein for nourishment of the next generation," said Pete Taylor, writing for *National Wildlife* magazine. Bummer to be a dude!

Several weeks after mating, the female, said Taylor, produces an egg sac, and six or seven weeks later, "hundreds of tiny spiderlings hatch to begin the cycle anew." After a few weeks, the young disperse to take up their lives. As tarantulas mature, they molt several times, each time shedding their old exoskeleton for a new one. The males may live for several years, the females, for several decades. The name 'tarantula' apparently originates in the 14th century, in the Italian city of Taranto, where people felt compelled to dance the wildly erotic "Tarantella" if bitten by a spider.

In nature, the life span of male tarantulas may be measured in a matter of weeks, days, hours, or minutes, according to the *Encyclopedia of Garden Plants*. They have no interest in anything other than finding a mate.

Like all tarantulas, they are harmless to humans and most pets (e.g., dogs and cats). Their venom is of no medical significance, and contrary to popular belief, nobody has ever died from such a bite; most people compare the bite to that of a bee sting and experience no lasting ill-effects other than mild to moderate pain and slight swelling at the site of the bite.

Some people find these spiders and decide that they would like to keep them as pets. Understand, they can be short-lived and males will wear themselves out literally to pieces trying to get away in order to find a female.

On their TV specials, National Geographic illustrated the methods used by some Amazonian peoples to hunt and cook tarantulas. The Goliath bird-eater tarantula (*Theraphosa blondi*) is considered a delicacy by the indigenous Piaroa of Venezuela. Another appearance of the tarantula as food was made on Anthony Bourdain's cable TV food show *"A Cook's Tour."* Odd to our tastes, but true! Wikipedia informs us that fried tarantulas are also considered a delicacy in Cambodia.

Unique Habitats

Ice Caves

ICE CAVE MELTING

I just watched "*Sunday Morning*" on CBS, and they were showing the Cherry Blossoms in Washington D.C., labeled as a sure sign of spring. The melting that takes place in the "Ice Caves" in Taos Canyon are Northern New Mexico's "sure sign of spring" and every bit as beautiful as far as I'm concerned.

Although water itself can neither be created nor destroyed (that's the 1st Law of Thermodynamics), its usefulness and availability can be. See Mr. Ernie Lopez, I *was* paying attention in ninth grade science class! Mr. Lopez was my favorite teacher at Taos Middle School back in the day. My understanding is he is still very much involved with the New Mexico State Science and Engineering Fair held annually, and who knows what else he's involved in.

A Sure Sign of Spring

According to Helen Fisher in *Water: No Longer Taken for Granted*, both the quality and quantity of water resources need to be protected for the nation's present and future generations. The current dry spell we are experiencing drives that point home. No resource is as vital to the West's urban centers, agriculture, industry, recreation, scenic beauty, and environmental conservation as its "liquid gold"—water.

Throughout the history of the West, battles have raged over who gets how much of this precious resource and when. The fundamental controversy is one of distribution, combined with conflicts between competing interests over the use of available supplies. Simply put: supply and demand.

Precipitation (rain, snow, and sleet) is the main source of all freshwater supplies. The amount of precipitation largely controls the availability of surface water and groundwater. Runoff refers to water that is not immediately absorbed into the ground and runs off into lower lying areas or surrounding lakes and streams. Runoff is the primary measure of a region's renewable water supply. In addition to rain, a large share of the West's runoff comes from the melting of mountain snowpacks, which are essentially huge reservoirs of frozen water that slowly release their supplies during the spring and summer.

To 'seep' means to pass, flow, or ooze gradually through a porous surface, according to the Merriam-Webster Dictionary. This is what we have at the "Ice Cave" in Taos Canyon. A spring is a source of water that issues from the ground. And a bog is wet spongy ground created by any of the above. Clear as mud?

Moss and Lichens

MOSS AND LICHENS

What are lichens? Lichens are 'dual organisms.' Every lichen is a partnership between members of two different kingdoms that live together in a special, mutually beneficial relationship. This is called a *symbiosis.* Each lichen is made up of a fungus and algae (green or blue-green). Mycology is the study of lichens; the publication *Mycology* describes almost 20,000 different lichens.

The fungus protects the algae from the harsh world outside, and provides them with water and mineral nutrients. The algae make their own food by photosynthesis, and leak some of this food, which is then absorbed by the fungus (which cannot make its own food). This partnership is so tough and self-reliant that lichens can grow in places like bare rock in deserts, or in this case, bare rock in a rock shelter at about 8,200 feet elevation.

Dual Organisms

When it is too dry, too hot, or too cold, lichens go into a state of suspended animation until conditions improve. Since algae make up only about 5 percent of each lichen, and algae are out of action for much of the time, you can imagine that lichens grow *very* slowly—only a few millimeters per year. Those who know me would compare it to my facial hair! The lichens make up for this by living for *centuries*, or in a few cases, even millennia.

Now let's talk about other simple plants, for example, moss. Mosses are a botanical division (phylum) of small, soft plants that are typically 0.4 to 4.0 inches tall, and commonly grow close together in clumps or mats in damp shady locations. The "Ice Cave" in Taos Canyon is a good example. They do not have flowers or seeds, but reproduce using spores. Most mosses rely on wind to disperse the spores. In the genus *Sphagnum*, the spores are projected by compressed air and the spores are accelerated to about 36,000 times the earth's gravitational pull.

In many mosses, green vegetation can break off and form new plants without the need to go through the cycle of fertilization. This is a means of *asexual reproduction*, and the genetically identical plants can lead to the formulation of *clonal populations*. Since mosses have no vascular system to transport water through the plant or waterproofing systems to prevent water from evaporating, they usually prefer a damp environment in which to grow and a surrounding of liquid water to reproduce. I said it once, I'll say it again: *Ain't nature grand!*

Epiphytes

EPIPHYTES

So what exactly is an epiphyte, you might ask? An epiphyte is a plant that grows on another plant and depends on it for support but *not* food, or sometimes it is dependent on some other object for support, such as a building or telephone pole. An epiphyte gets its moisture and nutrients from the air and rain, and sometimes from debris accumulating around it, hence its name "air plant." When Tarzan swung from tree to tree in the jungle, he swung from an epiphyte. Like my dad says, *"Cada chango en su columpio,"* or "Every monkey on his own swing."

Epiphytes account for 10 percent of all plant species and are found in many different plant groups, including begonias, bromeliads, orchids, ferns, lichens and mosses. Since they have no roots in the ground, epiphytes use special adaptations to obtain and store water and nutrients. Some epiphytes, particularly the bromeliads, capture water in the small cavities at the base of their overlapping leaves. These "tank epiphytes" provide a source of water to many other forest critters.

The Air Plant

An epiphyte does *not* derive any nourishment from its support and is thus distinguished from a parasite, which derives its nourishment from its host. Epiphytes, though found in all climates, are most numerous in the moist tropics. In Northern New Mexico, which averages 12.3 inches of precipitation per year, an Engelmann spruce (shown here) or Douglas fir tree in an old-growth forest stand is as close as we get to "the moist tropics."

As I said earlier, many plant families contain epiphytes. Probably the best-known epiphyte, the Spanish moss, is a bromeliad. I first got to know this plant when I went to law enforcement training in Georgia in the mid-1980s, where I saw it in the Okefenokee Swamp. *'Okeefenokee'* comes from the Hitchiti Creek Language meaning "waters shaking."

Because of its aerial environment, the epiphyte is frequently subjected to a lack of moisture; therefore, it developed the drought-resistant characteristics of dry-land plants. For example, the leaf surface is reduced in area and is covered with fine hairs to reduce the loss of water through transpiration. The leaves may also be modified as water-storage organs, as in the fleshy orchids, or with the leaves arranged so as to trap water, as in bromeliads.

The root system of epiphytes may consist partly of structures that anchor the plant and partly of aerial roots that are modified to absorb moisture when available from dew, rain, and moist substrates. The aerial roots also absorb nutrients from any dust and debris that are washed upon them. These roots are covered with a spongy tissue, the velamen, which also holds water. In some epiphytes these roots contain chlorophyll and carry on photosynthesis. This is either a *'ain't nature grand'* statement or TMI (too much information). *OK, OK, I'll quit already!*

Ecotone, Valle Vidal

ECOTONE

One of my favorite classes in college was Ecology. It was something I could relate to and besides it was a required class for Wildlife Science majors. I found a book at the Taos Municipal Library entitled *Ecology: A Bridge Between Science and Society* by Eugene P. Odum. In the epilogue of the book it states "…we must merge the 'study of the house' (ecology) and the 'management of the house' (economics), and our ethics must be extended to include environmental as well as human values." Sounds a lot like *A Sand County Almanac* written by Aldo Leopold in 1949 where he wrote that land as "a community is the basic concept of ecology, but that land is to be loved and respected is an extension of ethics.

The Valley of Abundant Life

An ecotone, then, is the boundary between one habitat type and another habitat type, such as: meadow and water, spruce forest and grass, aspen forest and shrub field, and so on. One of the best examples of an ecotone that I could think of is seen in the Valle Vidal on the Carson National Forest. The Valle Vidal (aka "the Valle") has all three examples described above, and then some.

The Valle was established in 1985 and is managed by the Carson National Forest. It was set aside by the U.S. Forest Service "to manage the unit to protect its prime resource—its wildlife." Located in the Sangre de Cristo Mountains of Northern New Mexico, the Valle is home to a magnificent array of wildlife, including 60 species of mammals, 33 species of reptiles and amphibians, and 15 varieties of fish.

In addition to being home and calving grounds to the State's largest elk herd, the Valle contains mountain lion, turkey, buffalo, mule deer, and the native Rio Grande cutthroat trout.

The Valle was acquired from Pennzoil Oil Company, and in December 2006, President Bush signed legislation that prohibited oil drilling and mining in the Valle Vidal. Think about it. President Bush, an oilman by trade, thought it important enough and unique enough to protect the Valle.

An ecotone, then, is not simply a boundary or an edge; the concept assumes interaction between two or more different habitats, which results in the ecotone having properties that do not exist in either of the adjoining habitats by themselves. Sometimes ecotones are populated by more kinds and larger numbers of birds and game animals than can be found in the interior of the adjoining habitats. This is called "Edge Effect" and is one of the basic tenets of ecology. Complexity equals diversity.

I'll give you an example: an elk likes to graze in open meadows where food is abundant, but it likes to have hiding cover close by in case a predator wanders by. So a setup like Valle Vidal is just what the doctor ordered. That is why edge habitat is so important and so heavily sought by critters of every sort.

Migration

"Wild beasts and birds are by right not the property merely of people of today, but the property of the unborn generations, whose belongings we have no right to squander..."

— THEODORE ROOSEVELT

SANDHILL CRANE MIGRATION

We will look at three examples of local animal(s) migration including migratory birds, kokanee salmon, and the bald eagle. Most of us have some familiarity with migration in general, in particular bird migration. Wedges of geese flying south in the fall, songbirds appearing in the spring, salmon returning to their native streams to spawn. Animals usually migrate to exploit a habitat that is more bountiful. When conditions deteriorate—temperature drops, food runs out—migratory animals leave.

But how do we know if an animal is migrating or just looking for the next rich patch of food? In *Nature's Flyers*, David Alexander writes that migrating animals tend to show distinctive behaviors, like storing up fat reserves, moving along straight paths, and stopping to feed less often. The ability to fly is a great advantage for migrants, regardless of the distance traveled. The Arctic Turn holds the long-distance migration record for birds, traveling between Arctic breeding grounds and the Antarctic each year. Other birds may only fly to lower elevations on the same mountain in the winter.

Switching gears, let's look at the Kokanee salmon, a species you wouldn't think of as migratory. Kokanee is a land-locked salmon, meaning it retains all the behaviors of a sea-going salmon, but there is no ocean to complete its journey. That doesn't stop the Kokanee though. Kokanee (*Oncorhynchus nerka*) are sockeye salmon that spend their entire lives in fresh water, and are usually found in lakes that have either limited or no access to the ocean. Kokanee tend to be smaller in size than sockeye, the average being 10- to 18-inches long and weighing 1 to 4 pounds. The kokanee in Eagle Nest Lake are a good example.

They exhibit similar markings and coloration to sockeye salmon, with bright silver sides, bluish-black tops and white bellies. Before spawning, kokanee will turn bright red with green heads; the males will also develop a humped back and hooked jaw. Kokanee are native to Alaska, British Columbia, Pacific Northwest United States, Siberia and Japan, but they have been introduced into lakes and hatcheries all over North America.

There and Back Again

After reaching maturity around 3 or 4 years of age, Kokanee return to the streams where they were born, and spawn between August and November. Spawning may occur in an inlet stream or on gravel beds on the lakeshore. The adult fish die within days of spawning. The fertilized eggs will develop in the gravel for one to two months and emerge as alevins. The alevins will remain in the gravel until they have consumed their attached yolk sac and then emerge from the gravel as fry, or as my friend would call them, "baby fish," and swim downstream to the lake where they will develop into mature adults and begin the life cycle all over again. *Ain't nature grand!*

Finally, the Rocky Mountains have always been a haven for the bald eagle (*Haliaeetus leucocephalus*), and this easily recognized bird is a source of inspiration and wonder to tourists and locals alike. Bald eagles also cast their spell on native peoples as this widespread raptor is symbolically represented in their totems, headdresses and folklore.

The decision to select the bald eagle as the United States' national emblem was adopted in 1782 because of its perceived fierce demeanor. Smaller bald eagles can be seen beginning early autumn on the Rio Grande according to river rangers with the U.S. Bureau of Land Management, but the larger migrant eagles won't arrive until sometime in November from Alaska, Canada and the Northwest Territories.

The bald eagle does have a spectacular "aerial courtship dance" by the male and the female birds, by locking talons and falling from the air with a series of somersaults. I got to see this courtship dance when I was working at Trempealeau National Wildlife Refuge in Wisconsin in the 1980s. It was the coolest thing I had ever seen!

The bald eagle is very easily distinguished from other birds by its very large size (30 to 43-inch body, 5.5 to 8-foot wingspan), white head and tail, dark brown body, yellow beak and feet, and yellow eyes. Ninety percent of the eagle's diet is fish, supplemented by small birds and mammals like prairie dogs, ground squirrels and rabbits. The immature bald eagle can be distinguished from the golden eagle by its unfeathered yellow legs, whereas a golden eagle has heavily feathered legs and feet down to its toes.

Palisades Sill

(*Porphyritic dacite sill*)

PALISADES SILL

The Palisades Sill is a fine-grained porphyritic dacite sill that formed spectacular cliffs and palisades in the Cimarron River canyon between Eagle Nest and Cimarron, New Mexico. What exactly is a 'porphyritic dacite sill,' you might ask?

According to the *Intermediate Thorndike Barnhart Dictionary*, dacite is a form of igneous rock, meaning that it was formed by the cooling of melted rock. It is light in color and is predominately composed of silica, feldspar, and one or more other minerals. In this particular case the color is light red to yellowish.

Nature's Palace

In melted form, called magma, dacite is an extremely sticky, thick-molten material like heavy syrup or glue, hindering it from moving very far away from its point of eruption before it cools and solidifies. The substance is, therefore, highly involved in the creation of thick volcanic domes, such as can be found in the Mount St. Helens volcano in Washington state.

Porphyritic means the igneous rock has large crystals scattered in a mass of smaller minerals, like Feldspar. Feldspar is a kind of crystalline mineral containing aluminum, silicon, and various other elements. Feldspars are the most abundant minerals in the earth's crust. They are used in making glass and pottery, as I learned from my father-in-law "Paisano," who was a professional glassblower by trade in the good old days.

I remember when I ran the Manitou Experimental Forest in

Colorado, I produced a "History of Manitou" DVD, and while doing the research for it I learned that they used to make bombsights out of feldspar back in the World War II days. Who knew I'd ever have need to re-collect those little-known facts. I'll tell you what—wildlife biology is a lot more "intuitive" to me than geology!

Capulin Volcano National Monument

For weeks, earthquakes disturb the quiet of ice age woodlands near the dry Cimarron River in what will one day become northeastern New Mexico. Then, in a moment of geologic time, an especially violent tremor shakes the ground, and a fissure in the earth opens. Rumbling and hissing, steam and smoke surge into the sky, and glowing red magma bubbles to the surface and erupts in a curtain of fire. A river of lava flows slowly southeastward from the vent.

CAPULIN VOLCANO

This is the description of the geological events in Laurence Parent's booklet, *Capulin Volcano National Monument,* published by Western National Parks Association. As the first lava flow ends, more magma reaches the surface, propelled by rapidly expanding gases such as water vapor and carbon dioxide. The gas depressurizes and explodes glowing jets of molten lava into a fiery fountain. These lava droplets, or cinders, spray outward in graceful arcs and pile up around the vent.

Cinder Cone of Northeast New Mexico

Smaller particles of glassy lava, called volcanic ash, are blown a thousand feet into the air creating a lava rain. They darken the sky and cover everything with a gray blanket, as lightning slices the sky near the rim of a quickly growing lava cone. Larger chunks of lava called volcanic bombs, some weighing hundreds of pounds, are ejected from the vent. They twist and turn in flight, landing with solid thuds and rolling down the steep slopes of the cone.

At night glowing particles rise several hundred feet into the air like fireworks, illuminating the cinder cone and ash cloud with an unearthly red glow. Blue flames from burning gases flicker throughout the crater. Capulin Volcano is born.

A person must have a very active imagination to picture this chain of events, yet the proof of this scenario lies before you when visit Capulin Volcano National Monument. Even more breathtaking to me is the fact that every summer thousands upon thousands of *ladybugs* descend upon the crater. These small orange beetles with black spots cover rocks, trees, grass, logs, and just about everything that covers the volcano. My friend Diane and I were lucky enough to witness this migration of ladybugs in Colorado when we visited a fire tower called "Devil's Head" high above Denver.

Each spring, ladybugs catch the wind and float south from Capulin Volcano onto the eastern plains, sometimes as far as east Texas. After feasting on aphids, their favorite food, the adult insects lay their eggs. Newly hatched larvae also gorge themselves on aphids, and as their food supply runs out, this next generation rides the wind back to Capulin Volcano. *Ain't nature grand!*

El Malpais

EL MALPAIS

Located in northwestern New Mexico near Grants, "El Malpais" is Spanish for "the badlands," due to the extremely barren and dramatic volcanic fields that cover much of the Park. I visited the El Malpais National Monument Headquarters and learned that some of the oldest Douglas fir trees *(Pseudotsuga menziessii)* on the planet are living in the El Malpais Monument, although you wouldn't think it just looking at them. They are short, scraggly, rough-looking trees not more than the size of a tall shrub. In other words, nothing to write home about!

"The Badlands" of Northwestern New Mexico

Historically speaking, the area surrounding El Malpais was used for gathering resources like firewood, human settlement, travel by Native Americans and Spanish conquistadors, and pioneer exploration. Archeological sites that show these activities are abundant within the Park.

In the 1940s the Malpais lava field was one of eight candidate sites considered for the Manhattan Project to test detonate the first atomic bomb. However the Trinity Nuclear Test Site to the south was chosen to test the atomic bomb at White Sands Proving Ground. The Department of Defense did use El Malpais as a bombing range to train pilots during World War II. After the war, the U.S. Bureau of Land Management became the administrator of the area, and in 1987, President Reagan created El Malpais National Monument and designated it a unit of the National Park Service. Today it is jointly managed with nearby El Morro National Monument.

We can't talk about El Malpais without defining what a lava tube is. A lava tube is a natural conduit formed by flowing lava which moves beneath the hardened surface of a lava flow. Lava tubes can be actively draining lava like on the Big Island of Hawaii or it can be extinct like on El Malpais National Monument. On extinct lava flows the lava flow has ceased, and the volcanic rock has cooled and left a long, cave-like channel on the landscape.

In the words of Forrest Gump, *"That's all I have to say about that!"*

Plants

Rocky Mountain Penstemon

(*Penstemon strictus*)

ROCKY MOUNTAIN PENSTEMON

Also called "Rocky Mountain beardtounge," this is an evergreen perennial plant with multiple spires of large, royal blue to purple flowers rising above low mats of foliage. The two lobes of the tubular flowers' upper lips project forward over the lower lips' three deeply cut lobes. Very pretty flower, not something you would expect to see out in the wild.

The blooms of this flower can be seen from late May through June annually in Arizona, Colorado, New Mexico, Utah and Wyoming. These particular plants were seen in the Moreno Valley close to Eagle Nest, New Mexico. The penstemon belongs to Figwort family, Scrophulariaceae. My whole time in college I never did get the family name spelled right. And I am a fourth-grade spelling bee champ; that was my claim to fame! Go figure.

The Showy Flower

The two upper petals point straight along the tube, like a porch roof, hence the seldom-used "porch penstemon." It is found in piñon-juniper woods with Gambel oak, or in open areas like the Moreno Valley with Ponderosa pine and spruce-aspen forests, often associated with sagebrush. Because of its combination of showy flowers, tolerance for drought, and hardiness, Rocky Mountain penstemon is often grown as an ornamental flower in dry regions, the coldest being in Region 4 (-30 to -20 degrees Fahrenheit) as described in the *Encyclopedia of Garden Plants.*

Native Americans have long used penstemon for human and animal uses. The Navajo used it to increase the recovery rate of open flesh wounds by inhibiting inflammation, which then increases the muscular activity of new regenerative growth of tissues. Regionally, it has also been used for compresses, ointments, creams, balms, foot soaks, and bath herbs. Internally, it was boiled to produce a refreshing drink for internal injuries and coughs. Veterinarians have used it for sick or injured animals, externally for abrasions, flesh wounds, broken bones, and to prolong livestock growth and survival.

One of the largest collections of Penstemons in North America is found at the arboretum in Flagstaff, Arizona, which hosts a Penstemon Festival every summer. I am proud to say I attended this festival when I lived and worked in Flagstaff in 2011 and 2012.

Pasqueflower

(*Pulsatilla vulgaris*)

Pasqueflower is a low-growing perennial plant that forms clumps that spread over time. It is a member of the Ranunculaceae family, which is Latin for "little frog." The name was given to the family because a group of plants in this family grow where frogs live.

PASQUEFLOWER

The Easter Flower

The Pasqueflower has thick, stout stems that rise 6 to 8 inches off the ground, and on each stem is one flower with 5 to 8 petals. The range of color in the petals is from dark lavender to almost white with yellow stamens in the center. Below the flower, around the stem, is a leaf covered in silky hairs, as is the rest of the plant. The fruit of the plant is a plum that is "achenial," which means that one seed is attached to the ovary wall, like a strawberry seed. These characteristics make this species distinctive season long.

Why is the flower covered in hairs you may ask? Well, if your home was in the tundra, you would wear a fur coat too! One of the earliest spring bloomers, it pushes through snow and old weathered grass in well-drained soils, from the prairies to mountain meadows. The flower occurs at the top of Wheeler Peak (13,110 feet), as well as up Taos Canyon at about 8,500 feet.

According to Carl Schreier in *Field Guide to Wildflowers of the Rocky Mountains*, Pasqueflower is derived from the old form of the word *pasch* and refers to the feast of the Passover at Easter. The Pasqueflower is found from Alaska to Washington State, along the northern plains to Illinois, and along the eastern slopes of the Rocky Mountains to Texas.

Native Americans had many medicinal uses for this plant, including its primary use as a sedative and for treating coughs. Pasqueflower is highly toxic and produces toxins, which slow the human heart. So understandably, it should not be used without the supervision of a medical doctor.

Nodding Beggartick

(*Bidens cernua lanceolata*)

NODDING BEGGARTICK

Ralph Waldo Emerson once said, "A weed is a plant whose virtues have not yet been discovered." This can be said for the nodding beggar-ticks, also known as the tickseed and locally as Ania del Muerta. The taxonomic name is Bidens.

This family of plants has been described as 'chaotic,' and it is not clear how many plant taxa are included in its bounds. There are probably at least 150 to 250 species, with some estimates falling around 230 species. Bidens is a genus of flowering plant in the Aster family (Asteraceae). This is a perennial plant that in summer freely produces daisy-like, bright yellow flower heads and branching stems.

The Chaotic Plant

Two things stand out about this flowering plant. First is the profusion of bright yellow, daisy-like flowers. You know what I'm talking about if you've been virtually anywhere in Taos County in the month of August. Second is the intense aroma that these flowers emit.

Another common name for this plant is Spanish needles or stickseeds, and it's a very appropriate description if you ask me. The fruits of the tickseed are bristly and barbed, with two sharp "anchors" at the end. Bidens comes from the Latin *bis* meaning "two" and *dens* meaning "tooth." As the name implies, the seeds of the plant are two-toothed (zoochorous), and the seeds will stick to clothing, fur, feathers, dog-hair, and more and will that way be carried to new habitats. That is their principal means of dispersal. Again: *Don't ya just love nature!*

In *Weeds of the West*, the authors state the term "weed" does not always indicate that a plant is totally undesirable, or that it cannot be beneficial under certain situations. Such is the case with nodding beggarticks. Bees thrive on the nectar of the yellow flowers, and it makes for quite a visual feast to the eyes.

Historically speaking, Alfred Savinelli was telling me at the U.S. Forest Service Supervisor's office that the plant was used in funeral rituals during embalming so the smell of decomposition wouldn't run you out of the church. Mr. Savinelli wrote a book called *Plants of Power* that is available on Amazon and goes into greater detail about this and many other plants. I can now understand why the plant was called "Ania del Muertas" by the old-timers in Northern New Mexico. This same name was given to me by Trisha at Moby Dickens bookstore in Taos, so that's two independent sources!

Osha'

(*Ligusticum porter*)

OSHA'

A native of higher altitudes of the Rocky Mountains and the Southwest, the root of the osha' plant is a traditional Native American herb. Osha' is strictly a mountain plant and commonly found in deep moist soils rich in organic matter. The plant requires partial shade, and it is widely distributed in the Rocky Mountains and the high mountains of northwestern Mexico. It is most common in the upper limits of the subalpine zone, so in the southern part of its range, it grows at elevations from 7,000 to 10,000 feet.

Good for Whatever Ails You

Osha' is the single most widely used herbal medicine in New Mexico for virtually any problem. It is usually ingested as a tea. The root also has many talismanic values, considered effective in warding off rattlesnakes when carried or tied around the boots, acts as a good luck charm, and is supposed to ward off the effects of witches. Hey, I don't make this stuff up…I just report it! Pueblo Indians placed an osha root in acequias (ditches) to cut down on cutworms and other larvae.

In *Curandero: A Life in Mexican Folk Healing* by Eliseo "Cheo" Torres, the author states that "perhaps the most popular of all these high desert country plants, in terms of its use as a remedy, is osha', otherwise known as *chuchupate*." This plant seems to be regarded as a cure-all for a wide variety of maladies. Osha' root was historically used by Plains Indians for treatment of respiratory problems. The herb is sometimes combined with wild cherry bark, licorice root, or common mullein, and together made into a syrup and administered directly.

In *Secrets of the Sacred White Buffalo: Native American Healing Remedies and Rituals* by Gary Null, the author says to burn the osha' root and inhale the smoke for maximum results in clearing tight mucus. John Duncan, a local herbalist, told me a simple recipe for a medicinal honey is to grind osha' root and infuse it into honey for a winter *remedio.* John also suggests cutting the root into small pieces instead of grinding it to allow you to have pieces of honey-infused osha' to chew on.

Osha' is sometimes confused in the wild with poison hemlock; the difference between the two is that the osha' root is extremely 'hairy' and smells like incredibly strong celery. Osha' got the name "bear medicine" because it was noted by Native Americans and early settlers that bears would seek osha out when they first emerged from hibernation as a means to stimulate their appetite, as well as to chew it into a cud of sorts and then drip it down and rub it into their fur. Osha' also went by the common names Colorado cough root, Porter's wild lovage, Indian root, empress of the dark forest, and mountain ginseng.

Osha' is dependent on mycorrhizal fungi, and as such, attempts to artificially cultivate the plant outside of its native habitat have not been very successful. Again: *"Ain't nature grand!"* Virtually all commercially grown osha' is wild-harvested.

According to Tibo J. Chavez in *New Mexican Folklore of the Rio Abajo (Lower Rio Grande)*, Osha' de la Sierra is one of the most multi-used of the medicinal plants. It is used to treat wounds or sores; the dry root is chewed for stomach disorders and headaches, and it is mixed with other 'remedios' and applied to the chest or other parts of the body that ail you. Considered the wonder drug of the Rio Abajo, sheepherders and cowboys carried the dry root in their pocket as a medicinal kit.

Hinted at earlier, osha' grows in some areas of the mountainous West in the same habitat as poison hemlock and water hemlock, both highly poisonous members of the same family. Osha' can be easily distinguished from poison hemlock by its spicy celery odor, hair-like material on its root crowns, and its dark chocolate-brown, wrinkled root skin. Hemlock roots are white, fleshy and thin-skinned. They are typically heavily branched rather than carrot-like, and poison hemlock roots have little to no odor. The plants themselves smell musty or rank, while osha' leaves have an intense fragrance when bruised and are typically larger than those of poison hemlock.

Also, most poison hemlock plants have purple blotches or shading on the lower stems if they are fairly mature, but this is not always the case. Unlike its poisonous cousins, osha' does not tolerate overly moist soils, because it depends on mycorrhizal fungi, and it is never found growing in standing water! Nevertheless, osha' and poison hemlock can be found only a few feet apart from each other.

If the plant is growing in or near water in consistently moist soils, is approximately 1.5 feet tall, has purple blotches on the main stem, and is heavily branched with small umbels of white flowers, then it is probably poison hemlock and should be avoided.

"It may be that some little root of the Sacred Tree still lives. Nourish it then, that it may leaf and bloom and fill with singing birds. Hear me, not for myself, but for my people. I am old. Hear me that they may once more go back into the sacred hoop and find the good red road, the shielding tree." Black Elk, Oglala Sioux Holy Man and Medicine Man.

Trees

Chokecherry

(*Prunus virginiana*)

CHOKECHERRY BLOSSOMS

Most people refrain from eating any plant with the word "choke" in its name. Thus, the chokecherry is ignored by many who have access to its bountiful crop. That's a shame, for this delicious fruit deserves much more attention than it receives.

The black bears know better. In late August when the chokecherries ripen, the bruins seek out the trees, pulling them to the ground and stripping off their succulent fruit. In their zeal they often tear the small trees limb from limb to get at the cherries. Raccoons similarly feast on chokecherries, only they tend to do far less damage in the process. Chipmunks and deer mice pick them up, extract the stones (seeds), and leave the flesh behind. And of course, many species of birds avidly consume the fruit.

The food value of this widespread native cherry was not lost on the Native Americans. For many tribes (15 by my count), chokecherries were a staple food item, and for many tribes, chokecherry was the most important fruit in their diet.

Delicious but Overlooked Fruit

European settlers adopted the use of chokecherries in some areas, particularly in the northern Plains states and in the mountainous Southwest. Chokecherries have been traditionally used to make jam, jelly, wine and syrup. Chokecherry "leather" (fruit roll-ups) is still a unique, convenient, healthy, and tasty snack. Only very rarely are they still eaten dried as once was their primary use. In the literature on wild foods, chokecherries are often derided as 'second-rate' compared to their cousin the black cherry.

Actually, chokecherry gets its name from Spanish traditionalists that claim the fruit "makes you choke" when eaten out of season (i.e., not ripe). Chokecherries are dark purple when fully ripe. The cherries are borne in drooping clusters 3 to 6 inches long, each cluster containing 8 to 20 individual fruits.

I am told that chokecherries can also be identified from any other woody plant at any time of year by its distinctive scent, which one can experience simply by scratching the bark off a twig or small branch. I was always able to tell it was chokecherry by the white "birthmarks" along its stems. This is probably not a very scientific telltale feature, but it always worked for me!

Chokecherry is a riverside shrub. It tolerates wet or dry conditions and thrives upon disturbance. The chokecherry has been incredibly successful at colonizing old fields, roadsides, fencerows, and forest edges. Its frequency in such upland sites belies the fact that its principal natural habitat is riversides.

Piñon-Juniper Woodlands

PIÑON-JUNIPER WOODLANDS

On a large scale, the piñon–juniper woodlands are a major life zone (biome) of the Southwest. Piñon–juniper woodlands occupy about 47 million acres in the Western U.S. They are located in a wide area between desert or grassland and higher elevation coniferous forests. The geographic distribution includes the states of New Mexico, Arizona, Colorado, Utah, Nevada and west-central California. In piñon–juniper woodlands, precipitation is patchy at best, and ranges from about 14 to 18 inches per year.

There are eight species of true piñon-pine tree in the U.S. (*Pinus edulis*), and the most extensive area is in New Mexico, where piñon-pine is honored as the official state tree. Wildlife forage on both piñon nuts and juniper berries. Avian inhabitants include piñon jay, bushtit, wild turkey and Northern goshawk, whereas mammals include mule deer, jackrabbits, deer mouse and ground squirrels.

Lifeblood of Northern New Mexico

Perhaps the most important historical use of piñon *and* juniper trees occurred in the mid-1800s when silver was discovered in Nevada. The requirements for firewood and fuel to smelt the ore were staggering, and much of the area surrounding the mining towns were denuded for several miles around the town to meet the smelting demand.

Harvests of the piñon nut occur every four or five years in the late autumn. I fondly remember piñon-picking excursions. We had to *make sure* what we picked was actually a piñon nut and not a rabbit dropping! Ah, the simplicity of those days.

The Juniper tree (*Juniperous osteosperma*) is part of the pine (*Pinaceae*) family. Cedar trees are also in the Pinaceae family of trees, but are native to the countries of North Africa and Asia. Contrary to popular belief, true cedar trees have no varieties that are native to the U.S.. Some junipers are given the common name cedar, including *Juniperous virginiana*, the 'red cedar' that is widely used in cedar drawers. In fact, in the book *Trees of North America* by Christian Frank Brockman, the author explains that cedar trees were planted in the U.S. mostly for ornamental purposes. When the term "cedar tree" is used to describe native trees of America, it refers to a group of conifers or cone-bearing trees that have very fragrant wood. It is often used to make trunks to store sweaters or other valuable clothing. My friend Diane had just such a trunk that she stored sweaters in.

The red cedar, common to the Eastern US, is actually a juniper. There are three true cedar varieties, each having rich, brown-colored bark and ascending branches with pine needles in various shades of green. The seed cones of true cedar trees are usually produced every other year. Humans have utilized cedar trees over the centuries for boats, boxes, bowls, and baskets.

Juniper berries are a spice in a wide variety of culinary dishes, is a primary flavoring in gin, and juniper berry sauce is often a popular flavoring choice for quail, pheasant, veal, rabbit, venison and other meat dishes. Whatever it is called—cedar or juniper—its value for food, fuel, wood for shelter and utensils is unmistakable not only in the Southwest but throughout the world.

To sum up: does the tree have scale-like green "sprays" that are flattened into fanlike foliage, and does it have small cones or tiny pink flowers attached to the fanlike sprays? If so, you're probably looking at a cedar. Or: does the tree have berrylike, blueish, glaucous, bloomy cones on tips of shoots, and is the tree shape narrowly columnar with have spiny, needlelike leaves? If so, you're probably looking at a juniper (according to the Forestry section of *About.com*).

Eastern Cottonwood

(*Populus deltoids*)

EASTERN COTTONWOOD

When pioneers crossed the Great Plains on the Santa Fe or Oregon Trail(s), they often went for days without seeing a tree. No trees meant there wasn't any wood for cooking; dried bison dung was used for cooking fuel instead. No trees also meant no shade, and if you've ever been out in the Great Plains on a hot summer day, you know just how miserable that can be.

However, there is a tree that is well adapted to life on the prairie—the Eastern cottonwood tree. To the pioneers, it meant the possibility of finding wood and shade, and it also meant the chance of finding water, since this deciduous species likes to 'keep its feet wet,' so to speak. Cottonwood trees can be either male or female. It is the fluffy white seeds produced by the females during the early summer that gives the tree its name. The seeds are very small, just 1 millimeter wide by 4 millimeters long, which is remarkable considering that they can become one of the largest trees in North America, up to 100 feet high with massive trunks over 5 feet wide.

Monarch of the Plains

Trees had to survive prairie fires in order to live on the Great Plains; cottonwoods did this by typically growing on the edges of rivers and streams and by developing a very thick, corky bark to withstand fire. As their seeds are dispersed by the wind, many end up landing on the surface of water and are then stranded along the waterline on sandbars, islands and riverbanks. If the river level does not fluctuate too much, allowing the seeds to establish themselves, new monarchs of the plains will begin life.

Cottonwoods can live to be over 100 years old. They share the same shaking, shimmering leaves of all poplars and aspens, and the leaves turn a bright yellow in the fall, making a vivid contrast with the dark green conifers and clear blue skies of autumn. The center of the tree, called heartwood, typically rots from the larger limbs and trunk of a cottonwood. If a windstorm breaks one of these hollow branches off, providing access to the interior of the tree, they can provide homes for squirrels, raccoons, birds of all sorts, and even a hive of honeybees. *Ain't nature grand!*

The cotton produced by cottonwood trees only lasts two or three weeks and blows up to 5 miles away. That's some serious frequent flyer miles! Contrary to popular belief, the cottonwood pollen does not actually cause allergy symptoms.

As with aspen, the petiole (leafstalk) is flattened sideways so that the leaves "shake" in the wind. The subspecies in New Mexico, Colorado and west Texas is the Rio Grande Cottonwood (*Populus deltoides wislizeni*). The wood of cottonwood trees is coarse and of fairly low value, and is used to make pallets, shipping crates and similar purposes where a cheap but strong enough wood is suitable. Cottonwood does not dry well, rots quickly, and splits poorly (it is very "stringy"). It produces a low level of energy per unit of volume of wood.

There are some estimates that a mature cottonwood will use 200 gallons of water per day. In an arid state like New Mexico, that is a lot of water. If a cottonwood root is cut, it will "bleed" water for days until the cut heals.

Aspen

(*Populus tremuloides*)

ASPEN

Aspen is a deciduous tree native to cooler areas of North America and very familiar in Northern New Mexico. It is commonly called quaking aspen, "quakies," trembling aspen, and trembling poplar. There are even more common names, but you know me, I only go by scientific name, *Populus tremuloides*. My ninth grade science teacher, Mr. Ernie Lopez, taught me that.

The Quakies

Aspens have pale white bark, black "scars," and glossy green leaves that become golden yellow in the autumn, but can also turn red or orange, though rarely. The quaking aspens' claim to fame is that it is the most widely distributed tree in all of North America, being found from Canada to Central Mexico. The quaking or trembling of the leaves is due to the flexible, flattened petioles (leafstalks) that cause the leaves to "shake" when hit by the breeze. *Ain't nature grand!*

The aspen is a tall, fast-growing tree usually 65 to 85 feet tall at maturity, with a trunk 0.75 to 2.6 feet wide. The record aspen is 120 feet tall and 4.5 feet wide. I've personally seen aspens close to this size near Pagosa Springs, Colorado.

Aspen reproduce primarily through root sprouts, and extensive clonal colonies are common. Each colony is its own clone, and all the trees in the clone have identical characteristics and share a single root structure. If you've ever tried to transplant aspens you would know just what I mean. Aspens do produce seeds, but seldom grow from them. One of the reasons is that pollination is inhibited by the fact that aspens are either male or female, and large stands of aspen are usually all clones of the same sex. Even if pollinated, the tiny seeds are only viable for a short time as they lack a protective coating.

Beginning in 1996, scientists noticed an increase in dead or dying aspen trees. This accelerated through 2004, as debate spread among scientists over the causes. In a 'Science and Nature' article in the December 2008 issue of *Smithsonian Magazine*, research forester Dr. Wayne Shepperd stated that while the aspen trees have always been susceptible to numerous diseases and insect attacks, especially in old age, this was "totally different from anything we'd seen before." Dr. Shepperd, or "Wayno" as we referred to him, was our supervisor at the Rocky Mountain Research Station in Fort Collins, Colorado. Great boss and sharp as a tack!

By 2007, the grim phenomenon had a name—sudden aspen decline, or SAD—and the devastated acreage had more than doubled to 300,000 acres, with some 13 percent of Colorado's aspen showing declines. In many places, patches of bare and dying treetops are as noticeable as missing teeth, and some sickly areas stretch for miles.

Some aspen clones are thousands of years old—although the individual trees live 150 years at most. Hmmm, this sounds like a riddle doesn't it? Riddle: "What is over a thousand years old, but lives to be 150 years old at most?" Answer: An aspen clone. One especially large stand in Utah, known as "Pando," after the Latin for *'I spread,'* was recently confirmed by geneticists to cover 108 acres and is said to be the world's heaviest, largest and oldest living organism. I've said it once, and I'll say it again: *Ain't nature grand!*

The Moon

The Moon

THE MOON

Not my typical field of expertise or comfort level in describing the "mysteries of wildlife science," but what the heck? There is currently a full moon, and it caught my attention. Cheryl Nixon, a librarian at the Taos Public Library, was able to show me the books relating to the moon. A book that caught my eye was *Five Billion Vodka Bottles to the Moon* by Iosif Shklovsky, a Russian cosmonaut. It turned out to be *way* too technical for me to read, much less understand.

"When the Moon Hits Your Eye Like a Big Pizza Pie ..."

The patterns of the rising and setting of the sun, moon, and stars over the horizon played a central part in astronomy from prehistoric times well into our own era. The very language with which we today describe these events carries with it certain information that correlates with the cycles of growth in nature. An example of this is the term 'equinoxes'—when day and night are of equal length in spring and autumn.

I recall memories of night fishing at Charette Lake near Springer, New Mexico, where my three brothers and my dad each caught our limit of rainbow trout. And I remember the newspapers used to publish the lunar tables in the sports section. Putting two and two together, I realize now that fish activity, and wildlife for that matter, and the moon are closely linked. I don't understand the connection, but I know they are connected.

I also know that surveying for Mexican spotted owls and flammulated owls is best done at the full moon, although I suspect this is as much out of convenience as much as any other reason, because you can see better where you are walking in full moonlight. My main point is the influence the moon plays and its vital role in what we experience with wildlife and fish.

At full moon, the moon is behind the earth in space with respect to the sun, and as the sun sets, the moon rises with the side that faces the earth fully exposed to sunlight. The full moon that occurs closest to the autumnal equinox is commonly called the 'harvest moon', since its bright presence in the night sky allows farmers to work longer into the fall night. The full moon in October is referred to as the 'hunters' moon', and if you hunt, you'll understand why.

So what is a 'blue moon'? Because the time between two full moons doesn't quite equal a whole month, approximately every three years there are two full moons in one calendar month. The second full moon has come to be known as a blue moon. The next time two full moons occur in the same month will be July 2015; the most recent blue moon occurred in August 2012.

Blue moons are rare because the moon is full every 29.5 days, so the timing has to be just right to squeeze in two full moons in one calendar month. The timing has to be really precise to fit two blue moons into a single year; it can only happen on either side of the month of February, whose 28-day span is a short enough time span to have *no full moons at all* during the month.

The term "blue moon" has not always been used this way, however. While the exact origin of the phrase remains unclear, according to *Star Date Moon Phases* by the U.S. Naval Observatory, it does in fact refer to a rare blue coloring of the moon caused by high-altitude dust particles. Most sources credit this unusual event, occurring only "once in a blue moon" as the "forefather" of the colorful moon phase. Thoroughly confused?

Sources

Bibliographic Sources

Adams, Rick. *Bats of the Rocky Mountains*. University Press of Colorado, 2003.

Alexander, David. *Nature's Flyers: Birds, Insects, and the Biomechanics*. Johns Hopkins University Press, 2002.

Bailey, Vernon. *Mammals of the Southwestern United States*. Dover Publications, 1971.

Bowers, Nora and Rick & Kaufman, Kenn. *Mammals of North America* (Kaufman Focus Guides). Houghton Mifflin Harcourt, 2004.

Burt, William & Grossenheider, Richard. *A Field Guide To The Mammals*. Houghton-Mifflin, 1971.

Brickell, Christopher, ed. *Encyclopedia of Garden Plants*. MacMillan Publishing, 1992.

Brockman, Christian. *Trees of North America*. St. Martin's Press, 2001.

Brybycin, George. *Wildlife in the Rockies*. G.B. Publishing, 1982.

Chavez, Tibo. *New Mexican Folklore of the Rio Abajo*. Gannon Distributing, 1987.

Childs, Craig. *The Animal Dialogues*. Little Brown, 1997.

Christiansen, Per, Ph.D. *The Encyclopedia of Animals*. University of California Press, 2006.

Cornell Lab of Ornithology. *All About Birds*. Ithaca, NY, 2003.

Coulter et al. *Winging It: A Beginner's Guide to Birds of the Southwest*. University of New Mexico Press, 2004.

Davis, Al. *Tarantulas: A Complete Introduction*, T.F.H. Publications, 1987.

Deinlein, Mary. "Yellow-bellied Sapsucker: The Master Sap Tapper." *nationalzoo.si.edu* Smithsonian Migratory Bird Center, National Zoo Smithsonian Institute, August 2003. Web. 8 October 2014.

Dunning, Joan. *Secrets of the Nest*. Houghton-Mifflin, 1994.

Elman, Robert. *The Living World of Audubon Mammals*. Grosset & Dunlap, 1976.

Findley, J.S. *The Natural History of New Mexican Mammals*. University of New Mexico Press, 1987.

Fisher, Chris. *Birds of the Rocky Mountains*. Lone Pine Publishing, 1997.

Fisher, Helen. *Water: No Longer Taken for Granted*. Thomson Gale Publishing, 2004.

"Forestry." Education. *About.com*. n.d. Web. 14 Oct. 2014.

Forshaw, et al. *Birding*. The Nature Company Guides, 1994.

Harrison, Hal & Petersen, Roger. *A Field Guide to Western Birds' Nests*. Petersen Field Guides. Houghton-Mifflin, 1979.

Johnsgard, Paul A. *Hawks, Eagles and Falcons of North America*. Smithsonian Institution Press, 1990.

Leopold, Aldo. *A Sand County Almanac and Sketches Here and There*. Oxford University Press, 1949.

Ligon, J.S. *New Mexico Birds and Where To Find Them*. University of New Mexico Press, 1961.

Lott, Dale. *American Bison: A Natural History*. University of California Press, 2003.

Martin, Craig, ed. *Fly Fishing in Northern New Mexico*, University of New Mexico Press, 1991.

Marzluff, John & Angell, Tony. *In the Company of Crows and Ravens*. Yale University Press, 2005.

"Mission & History." *Wild Sheep Foundation.org* 4 September 2013. Web. 8 October 2014.

National Geographic Society. *Birds of North America*. National Geographic, 1987.

National Geographic Society. *Birds of North America, 2/e*. National Geographic, 1994.

NM State Dept. of Game & Fish. *New Mexico Game and Fish Wildlife Notes*. New Mexico, 1992.

Null, Gary. *Secrets of the Sacred White Buffalo; Native American Healing Remedies and Rituals*. Prentice Hall, 1998.

Odum, Eugene. *Ecology: A Bridge Between Science and Society*. Sinaur Associates, 1997.

Parent, Laurence. *Capulin Volcano National Monument*. Western National Parks Assoc., 1991.

Pattie, Fisher & Hartson. *Mammals of the Rocky Mountains*. Lone Pine Field Guide, 2000.

Peterson, David. *Among the Elk*, Northland Publishing, 1988.

Price, Alice. *Cranes–The Noblest Flyers*. La Alameda Press, 2001.

Reader's Digest Editors. *Book of North American Birds*. Reader's Digest, 1990.

Rue, Leonard. *Game Birds of North America*. Outdoor Life. 1973.

Sams, Jamie & Carson, David. *Medicine Cards*. Bear and Company, 1998.

Savage, Candace. *Bird Brains: The Intelligence of Crows, Ravens, Magpies, and Jays*. Sierra Club, 1995.

Savinelli, Alfred. *Plants of Power: Native American Ceremony and the Use of Sacred Plants*. Book Publishing Company, 2002.

Sharp, Jay. "Tarantula." Insects. *Desert USA*. n.d. Web. 8 October 2014.

Shklovsky, Iosif. *Five Billion Vodka Bottles to the Moon: Tales of a Soviet Scientist*. Norton, 1991.

Schreier, Carl. *Field Guide to Wildflowers of the Rocky Mountains*. Homestead Publishing, 1996.

Sternberg, Dick. *Fly Fishing for Trout in Streams*. Cy DeCosse Inc., 1996.

Sterry, Paul & Small, Brian. *Birds of Western North America*. Princeton University Press, 1990.

Streit, Taylor. *Instinctive Fly Fishing*. Globe Pequot Press, 2012.

"Tarantula." Wikipedia.com n.d. Web. 8 October 2014.

Tekiela, Stan. *Birds of New Mexico, Field Guide*. Adventure Publications, 2003.

Thorndike, E.L. & Barnhart, Clarence. *Intermediate Thorndike Barnhart Dictionary*. Scott Foresman, Addison Wesley, 1997.

Torres, Eliseo & Sawyer, Timothy. *Curandero: A Life in Mexican Folk Healing*. University of New Mexico Press, 2005.

U.S. Fish & Wildlife Service. *Pronghorn*. October 2012.

U.S. Forest Service. *The True Story of Smokey Bear*. U.S. Dept. of Agriculture, 1960.

U.S. Naval Observatory. *Star Date Moon Phases*. n.d. Web. 9 October 2014.

Van Tighen, Kevin. *Antlered Animals of the West*. Altitude Publishing, 2001.

Wassink, Jan. *Mammals of the Central Rockies*. Mountain Press, 1993.

Weidensaul, Scott. *Living on the Wind: Across the Hemisphere with Migratory Birds*. North Point Press, 1999.

Western Society of Weed Science. *Weeds of the West*, 9/e. Western U.S. Land Grant Universities Cooperative Extension Services, 2001.

Willmer, Pat. *Pollination and Floral Ecology*. Princeton University Press, 2011.

Photo Credits

Photo attributions are indicated in parenthesis with each photo. Photos are public domain, licensed under Creative Commons as indicated in Wikipedia or by direct permission from the author.

Cover – American Marten – (Wikipedia: Public Domain)
p. 4 Peregrine Falcon – (Debbie Tapia)
p. 6 Wild Turkey – (Wikipedia: Vince Pahkala)
p. 8 Yellow-bellied Sapsucker – (Wikipedia: Dominic Sherony)
p. 11 Sandhill Crane – (Wikipedia: Steve Emmons)
p. 13 Osprey – (Wikipedia: Matt Edmonds)
p. 15 Western Tanager – (Wikimedia: Kati Fleming)
p. 16 Turkey Vulture – (Wikipedia: Mike Baird)
p. 18 The Birds and the Bees: Honeybee – (Wikipedia: Andy Murray)
p. 20 Scaled Quail – (Wikipedia: Clinton & Charles Robertson)
p. 22 Pinyon Jay – (Wikimedia: Peter Wallack)
p. 24 Chickadees (Wikipedia: Dan Pancamo)
p. 26 Mallard – (Wikipedia: Richard Bartz)
p. 28 Magpie – (Wikipedia: Linda Tanner)
p. 31 Raven – (Wikimedia: khyri)
p. 32 Hummingbird – (Wikimedia: Huzzar)
p. 35 House Wren – (Wikipedia: Public Domain)
p. 37 Black-headed Grosbeak – (Sandra Tapia)
p. 39 Dusky Blue Grouse – (Wikipedia: Public Domain)
p. 41 Hermit Thrush – (Wikipedia: Matt MacGillivray)
p. 43 Great Horned Owl – (Wikipedia: Greg Humemons)
p. 45 Flammulated Owl – (Dr. Brian Linkhart)
p. 47 Evening Grosbeak – (Wikipedia: Peter Wallack)
p. 49 Common Goldeneye – (Wikipedia: Dick Daniels)
p. 51 Cinnamon Teal – (Wikipedia: "Mike" Michael L. Baird)
p. 53 Cassin's Finch – (Wikimedia: Public Domain)
p. 55 Western Bluebird – (Wikipedia: Kevin Cole)

p. 57 Canada Goose – (Wikipedia: Daniel D'Auria)
p. 59 Great Blue Heron – (Wikimedia: Public Domain)
p. 61 Black-crowned Night Heron – (Wikipedia: Dick Daniels)
p. 63 White-tailed Ptarmigan – (Wikimedia: John Hill)
p. 65 American Robin – (Wikipedia: Dakota Lynch)
p. 68 Cliff Swallow – (Wikimedia: Cephas)
p. 72 Short-tailed Weasel – (Albert Ortega)
p. 74 American Marten – (Wikipedia: Public Domain)
p. 76 Antlers – (Wikimedia: Jim Richmond)
p. 78 Lesser Horseshoe Bat – (Wikimedia: F. C. Robiller)
p. 80 Bison – (Wikipedia: Public Domain)
p. 82 Black Bear – (Wikimedia: Cephas)
p. 84 Mule Deer – (Wikipedia: Dcrjsr)
p. 86 Mountain Lion – (Wikipedia: USFWS Mountain-Prairie)
p. 88 Raccoon – (Wikimedia: Harlequeen)
p. 90 Porcupine – (Wikipedia: Public Domain)
p. 92 Coyote Pup – (Wikipedia: Rebecca Richardson [Red~Star])
p. 94 Yellow-bellied Marmot – (Wikipedia: Paxson Woelber)
p. 96 Pika – (Wikipedia: Sevenstar)
p. 98 Pronghorn – (Zeke Tapia)
p. 100 Red Fox Cubs – (Wikipedia: Ken Billington)
p. 102 Bighorn Sheep – (Wikipedia: Kjaergaard)
p. 106 Rio Grande Cutthroat Trout – (Nick Streit)
p. 108 Northern Pike – (Wikipedia: Mitte)
p. 110 Rainbow Trout – (Wikimedia: Mike Anderson)
p. 113 Brown Trout – (Wikipedia: Public Domain)
p. 116 Western Tiger Swallowtail Butterfly – (Wikipedia: Kathy Zimmerman)
p. 118 Tarantula – (Wikimedia: João Coelho)
p. 122 Ice Caves Melting – (Wikipedia: Dave Bunnell)
p. 124 Moss and Lichens – (Wikipedia: Fredlyfish4)
p. 126 Epiphytes – (Wikipedia: Hans Hillewaert)
p. 128 Ecotone – (Wikipedia: Nicholas)
p. 130 Sandhill Crane Migration – (Wikimedia: USFWS)

p. 133 Palisades Sill – (Wikipedia: Billy Hathorn)
p. 135 Capulin Volcano – (Wikipedia: Public Domain)
p. 137 El Malpais – (Wikipedia: Bryce Chackerian)
p. 140 Rocky Mountain Penstemon – (Steve Tapia)
p. 142 Pasqueflower – (Wikipedia: brewbooks)
p. 144 Nodding Beggartick – (Wikipedia: Wibowo Djatmiko)
p. 146 Osha' – (Wikipedia: Jerry Friedman)
p. 150 Chokecherry Flowers – (Wikipedia: Public Domain)
p. 152 Piñon-Juniper Woodlands – (Steve Tapia)
p. 154 Eastern Cottonwood – (Wikipedia: Matt Lavin)
p. 156 Aspen – (Wikipedia: Daniel Schwen)
p. 160 The Moon – (Wikipedia: B. Tafreshi)

The Author

PHOTO BY TINA LARKIN

I began my 27-year career with the U.S. Fish and Wildlife Service as a Cooperative Education (COOP) student in Princeton, Minnesota working as a Refuge Manager Trainee. As a small-town boy from Taos, New Mexico, I was like a fish 'outta water! I was still a college student at New Mexico State University, this was simply a "Work Phase" of my education. The next Work Phase was as a Refuge Manager at Trempeauleau National Wildlife Refuge in Trempeauleau, Wisconsin. I then graduated from NMSU with a Bachelor's of Science Degree in Wildlife Science in 1987.

The good thing about the COOP Program is the Agency places you in a Permanent position if you successfully complete your COOP work phase(s), which I did! I was then placed at the Imperial National Wildlife Refuge in Yuma, Arizona and then transferred to the U.S. Forest Service in Enterprise, Oregon as a Zone Wildlife Biologist. I worked for the Wallowa Valley Ranger District, Hells Canyon National Recreation Area, and the Eagle Cap Wilderness Area in a "Zone" capacity. Toughest job I ever loved!

I then transferred to the Pikes Peak Ranger District as a District Wildlife Biologist in Colorado Springs, Colorado, where I spent 17 years! I loved the area, the job, and my career…I said it once, I'll say it again, "do what you love, and you'll never work a day in your life"! The last transfer I made was to Flagstaff, Arizona as a NEPA Writer.

I retired from government service in this position at the GS-11, Step 8 grade level after 27 years because of the progression of Multiple Sclerosis. However, teaching people about wildlife and nature is in "in my blood." That is the reason for *De La Tierra: The Natural World of Northern New Mexico*. I truly hope you will enjoy the book!

— Steve Tapia

www.ingramcontent.com/pod-product-compliance
Lightning Source LLC
Chambersburg PA
CBHW072133020426
42334CB00018B/1783
9780986270635